"I enjoyed this book, learned from it - and strongly
trying to succeed at the interface between business
John Elkington, Chairman, Volans, and co-aut
The Breakthrough Challenge: 10 W
Profits With Tomorrow's Bottom Line

"Business should help people learn how they can live better lives and lead
society to create the systems and technologies to do so. *CORE* is a great
guide to how business can take on that task."
Charles Leadbetter, author of *We-think*

"Timely, engaging valuable and practical."
Zahid Torres-Rahim, Founder, Business Fights Poverty

"The fictionalized story really grabbed me. It dramatically brings home the
new reality of extreme global connectivity."
Professor David Grayson CBE, Professor of Corporate Responsibility,
Cranfield School of Management, UK

"No business can prosper in the future without a clear purpose and here at
last is a practical management tool to turn a great theory into gritty reality."
Mike Barry, Director, M&S Plan A

"*CORE* is a really important piece of work. We need this kind of principled
clarity more than ever before."
Simon Anholt, founder, Good Country and the Good Country Index

"At a time when organisations are struggling to cope with the pace of
change, managers need a method to focus their best efforts. This book offers
precisely that."
Charles Arthur, former Guardian Technology Editor 2009–14, author of
Digital Wars: Apple, Google, Microsoft and the battle for the internet

"This is a great reflection on the movement beyond CSR to one that connects
business – through purpose – to the real issues our societies need to deliver
on. It's a great recipe for future success – and one that is much needed. It will
be a good practical reference for any organisation wanting to make a positive
difference."
Rachel Brown, CEO, New Zealand Sustainable Business Network

"There's been a lot of pontification about why businesses need to develop a social purpose but precious little insight on how they can go about it. Refreshingly Neil's done exactly that with this book – a must read for any business that wants to create social change."

Jilly Forster, founder, Forster Communications

"When you have a core idea at the heart of your business, as co-operatives tend to in focusing on member needs, there can be a richness of motivation and a special kind of empowered collaboration at work. Keep it simple and you can bring more people on board."

Ed Mayo, Secretary General, Co-operatives UK, and author of *Values*

CORE

At the core of the world's most admired businesses lies a powerful Single Organizing Idea. These organizations deliver sustainable economic and social benefit; they unite people, attract investment, inspire innovation, pioneer new efficiencies, and enjoy positive reputation.

Such businesses are admired but they remain a rare breed.

Though the tides of change are engaging the minds of business leaders, most are still trapped behind their brands and an approach to corporate social responsibility that is out of step with a connected society that increasingly questions 'who' these businesses really are and what drives their purpose.

This book is about how businesses can adopt a Single Organizing Idea and, more importantly, why they have to. Drawing on stories and case studies, and with reference to the UN's Sustainable Development Goals, its no-nonsense approach sets aside the ideals to confront the realities of business reform. It demonstrates the power and potential that a Single Organizing Idea can bring to any business prepared to take its head out of the sand and proactively respond to today's challenges.

Neil Gaught is what Malcolm Gladwell would call an outlier. Neil was born in Hertfordshire in the UK in 1963. Following a short spell in the British Army and an even shorter one in the French Foreign Legion he completed his education at the London College of Printing where he gained a BA(Hons) in Graphic Design. A year after graduating he founded his first business, a London-based design consultancy. Having successfully run the business for ten years he sold it to a marketing company before joining WPP's largest global brand consultancy, Enterprise IG. There he took a leading role on a variety of high profile branding projects for Merrill Lynch, DeBeers, Andersen, Scottish Power, BG Group and Standard Chartered Bank, among others.

In 2003 Neil and his young family moved to New Zealand for the adventure. Following three years with the country's leading agency DesignWorks, Neil re-established his independent consultancy status. Since then he has advised a wide variety of organizations, ranging from international NGOs and energy, manufacturing and infrastructure corporates to tech start-ups, global faith based organizations and government institutions across Asia Pacific, Europe, Africa and the USA.

Neil is married with three children and lives in the countryside near London with two dogs, a cat and four nervous chickens.

CORE
How a Single Organizing Idea Can Change Business For Good

Neil Gaught

Foreword by Jonathan Glennie,
Director, Ipsos Sustainable Development
Research Centre

LONDON AND NEW YORK

First published 2018
by Routledge
2 Park Square, Milton Park, Abingdon, Oxon OX14 4RN

and by Routledge
711 Third Avenue, New York, NY 10017

*Routledge is an imprint of the Taylor & Francis Group,
an informa business*

© 2018 Neil Gaught

British Library Cataloguing-in-Publication Data
A catalogue record for this book is available from the British Library

Library of Congress Cataloging-in-Publication Data
A catalog record for this title has been requested

ISBN: 978-1-78353-786-0 (hbk)
ISBN: 978-1-78353-785-3 (pbk)
ISBN: 978-1-78353-787-7 (ebk)

Typeset in Sabon
by Saxon Graphics Ltd, Derby

In memory of Fred

Contents

This book has three distinct parts. You will get the most out of it by starting from the beginning but it has been designed so that you can go straight to the part that interests you most.

Foreword

With his book, *Core: How a Single Organizing Idea Can Change Business for Good*, Neil Gaught has bolstered the case for a radical rethink of how businesses are managed in the 21st century and added significantly to the debate about modern capitalism.

The growing realisation that companies can be a force for social and environmental benefit at the same time as turning a healthy profit is surely one of the most exciting ideas of our time. It is not new, but it seems to have been forgotten, certainly in the last few decades. On the right of the political spectrum, maximizing profit is seen as the main value businesses contribute to society; meddling with this simple objective by introducing social and environmental issues could undermine growth and jobs. In fact, maximizing profit for shareholders is a legal obligation in many countries. Meanwhile, on the left, the profit motive is held in high suspicion, but so is any attempt to muddy the clear dividing lines between the public sector, which is accountable for social progress, and the private sector, which is not. Although coming at it from different perspectives, both left and right thus share the same minimalist understanding of business.

But such a limited vision for the role of the private sector is on its way out as capitalism is rethought. Positive social impact is not the preserve of the public sector, nor are private companies the only purveyors of environmental damage. Both sectors are capable of making a huge contribution or creating lasting harm. In most countries, waiting for the public sector to become accountable and effective enough to successfully regulate the actions of private companies would mean a long wait indeed.

My career working with communities on the wrong side of globalisation has made me healthily sceptical about CSR (corporate social responsibility). Seeing the negative impacts of large mining, oil and agriculture companies on communities and the environment, I have viewed much CSR as marketing dressed up as charity, often paid for out of clever tax arrangements. But over the years I have learnt to be equally wary of flowery promises made by politicians and public sector leaders. In most countries there is just as much money to be made in politics and NGOs as there is in business. Society cannot rely on the public sector alone to safeguard its values.

There are brilliant people in all sectors of society, people committed to making a lasting and profound difference. Engaging with business as a crucial driver of positive change, while heretical for the theorists on left and right, is the only meaningful strategy for those who want to change the world for the better. Fortunately, more and more companies are demonstrating that the supposed tension between making money and making a difference is unsubstantiated. It could, in fact, be the opposite of the truth. The best businesses explicitly set out to contribute to society, now often in the context of the new Sustainable Development Goals (SDGs), and to live out authentically held values. That is increasingly what is expected of them by customers, employees and investors alike.

But it can be a nerve-wracking process, especially for business leaders schooled in a the more traditional dichotomy between private and public, and wary of taking risks. So how can it be done? That is the question Neil seeks to answer in this substantial addition to the debate. He joins the list of critics heralding the end of the era of CSR. As he says, identifying the odd win-win is not radical enough. And in the digital age, there is no more time for spin and greenwash. Businesses need to change in a more fundamental way, and Neil's idea of a Single Organizing Idea (SOI) is compelling.

I worked with Neil some years ago assessing the future strategy of a major international NGO, and the meticulous and pragmatic nature of his thinking, coupled with his ambition and idealism for what is achievable (usually far beyond what his clients might think possible) is evident throughout this book. Generously, Neil shares a lifetime of business consulting experience in a condensed how-to list for revealing and building a strategy around the SOI. And he does it in an eminently readable way, introducing anecdotes and ideas from leaders and ordinary people in business, academia and civil society to bring the argument to life. The opening fictional story not only helps pin down the central theme of the book, it is also a surprisingly gripping read!

Only by challenging long-held theories about the limitations of what the private sector can achieve, can we build a new economic model for a new century. If the business case for doing good is so compelling, why are so many companies still acting like it isn't, ignoring ethical practices and preferring a quick buck? Sure, there are powerful incentives in play that need to be challenged by public policy change. But perhaps it is also down to a lack of vision among business leaders. Perhaps they find it hard to shrug off what they have been educated to think. Rather than being bent on regressive behaviours, perhaps it's just that no-one has shown them a different way.

And that's why Neil's book is important. Thankfully, most people want to do the right thing. By making a compelling argument that doing so is compatible with business growth, and by setting out concrete steps to get from A to B, this book makes a valuable and original contribution.

Jonathan Glennie Director,
Ipsos Sustainable Development Research Centre

Introduction

The Country Director was in full flow now. She radiated passion and intensity through every word she delivered. The sheer belief expressed in her eyes lived up to the vivid portrait the senior management team back in Washington DC had painted of Lana Abu-Hijleh, the woman they nicknamed "The Queen of Palestine".

"We will never leave these people, we will always be here with them—we are here for good."

As she uttered these words a spontaneous sense of both euphoria and relief hit me. This was it—this was what I had been searching for.

I was "on a mission" as they say in the international development sector. This time for a global NGO with a new CEO at its helm.

Pretty much everything in the NGO's world had changed. While his predecessor had benefited from unprecedented levels of funding following the 9/11 terror attacks, the new CEO was having an altogether bumpier ride. The 2008 global financial crisis, new types of competition, new political masters, new technology and a new generation of people with fresh ideas ensured that questions about identity, role and value, previously left skulking in the long grass, now needed to be answered. My mission was to help find those answers.

Like many previous missions it took me on a journey of discovery. In this instance across four continents and into the offices of government ministries, behind the locked doors of embassies, to the air conditioned sanctuaries of multilateral institutions and global corporations, to the simple workplaces of civil society organizations, and into the homes, schools and hospitals of some of the world's poorest people. Before I sat down with Lana that day I had engaged with over two hundred people in one way or another. I simply wanted to know the fundamental truth of this NGO. And Lana nailed it.

Consequently, on September 18, 2012, the Cooperative Housing Foundation changed its name after 60 years to Global Communities. Below the name it proudly presented its marketing strap-line: "Partners for Good". But this isn't just a strap-line. It's a powerful statement of intent. An invitation to unify. A rallying call and a reference point against which everything Global Communities does, every new initiative it considers and every result it achieves is measured. "Partners for Good" is a powerful Single Organizing Idea that will continue to catalyse change and help the organization transition and adapt to the needs of the 21st century.

That's what a Single Organizing Idea does. But so what if an NGO dedicates itself to doing good? That's largely what NGOs are there for in the first place, right?

This book is about how commercial businesses can also adopt a Single Organizing Idea, and more importantly why they have to.

In it I'm setting idealism aside to demonstrate the power and potential that a Single Organizing Idea can bring to business, and how identifying, defining and aligning with such an idea could effect changes that not only deliver competitive advantage but benefits to society as well.

The tides of change may have engaged the minds of business leaders such as Indra Nooyi (the CEO of PepsiCo, who launched her Performance with Purpose strategy in 2006 and thinks corporates need to catch up with NGOs—although that may not be achieved through advertising!*). However, the reality is that most commercial entities—the mainstream—have yet to identify what their actual purpose is or what value they deliver beyond the often undifferentiated products or services they provide.

The truth of most businesses is hidden behind their brand and an approach to branding which is out of touch with audiences who want to understand who they really are. Identifying, defining and aligning a business with a Single Organizing Idea (SOI) can change that and at the same time potentially help change the world. And it's a necessary change.

The private sector and many of the colossal corporations that dominate it realized some time ago that we can't indefinitely keep plundering the finite resources of our planet—they're already running out. We can't indefinitely keep shifting activity to lower wage economies—soon there won't be any left. We can't keep widening the wealth gap because it continually diminishes the number of consumers who can afford our products. Capitalism is running out of options.

At the same time, societal expectations of business are changing. People no longer want to engage with organizations whose sole purpose is to sell us things and make a profit. That seems vulgar and unattractive now. Society expects more. It gets behind organizations that are perceived to be forward-thinking and actively engaged with the big issues and the topics we care about. Conversely, the businesses that seem oblivious or aren't forward-thinking enough are likely to be penalised with increasing frequency.

Businesses can't keep *pretending* to be benign to their employees, their suppliers and the planet if they're not. They operate in a world saturated by social media that now exposes bad behaviour, or indeed any behaviour that doesn't contribute to the greater good. And when businesses aren't perceived

---

*   See: www.youtube.com/watch?v=AfCiV6ysngU

as contributing to the greater good they can no longer attract and retain high quality employees or investors.

Likewise, businesses can no longer succeed in the long term selling products and services that underperform because, again, social media spreads the word and businesses are being held to account like never before.

In response to these challenges, a sizable number of academics, consultants and commentators have formulated and published their own thoughts about what to do next. There's a wide spectrum of ideas, but among them a lot of consensus around the fact that businesses of all sizes need to think hard about their fundamental purpose.

In essence, many are saying that businesses need to revisit the idea that their primary reason for existing is to deliver short-term profits to a relatively small number of shareholders. Instead—and this is already happening— businesses should re-orientate to achieve profit at the same time as they fulfil a societally useful purpose. In other words pursue a profit and social purpose agenda.

What does profit and purpose look like? Well, here's a simple example. I can make money selling coconut water. If in addition I pay my producers a bit more it ensures they can invest in more productive and sustainable agricultural practices. I might even spend money to help them do so.

The good news is that it's a win-win all round. It's good for me because it shores up my supply chain, so I get greater continuity of supply. Meanwhile my customers benefit from a healthy, delicious product. My suppliers and their communities benefit from agricultural practices which preserve their environment. My community benefits because I'm providing people with jobs and wages. My shareholders are fine too. Investment in the community has been based on a business calculation that satisfies the usual business investment criteria and delivers a return on investment (ROI) that will deliver stable, long-term income. This is particularly appealing to the long-term type of investor I'm specifically looking to attract. I don't want investors who are only interested in short-term, risky investments.

Of course this is an easy example. In reality it's not at all clear to most businesses what they can do, or how they can change.

In January 2016, at the World Economic Forum held in Davos, the Business and Sustainable Development Commission (BSDC) was launched by proactive global business leaders and civil society organizations, financially backed by a group of governments and foundations. As promised, one year later the Commission delivered its inaugural report to the class of Davos 2017. In it they laid out the economic advantages businesses would reap from putting social purpose at their core and achieving the United Nations Sustainable Development Goals (SDGs):

> The business case for sustainable development is strong already... it opens up new opportunities and big efficiency gains; it drives innovation; and it enhances reputations. With a reputation for sustainability,

companies attract and retain employees, consumers, B2B customers and investors, and they secure their license to operate. That's why sustainable companies around the globe are thriving and delivering attractive returns to shareholders.[1]

The report lists 60 market opportunities across four economic systems (food and agriculture, cities, energy and materials, health and well-being), related to the SDGs and backed its findings with figures: "380 million jobs will be created achieving the Global Goals and at least US$12 trillion in opportunities." It sets out six actions business leaders can take "to capture your share of this prize." Action number 2 is "Incorporate the Global Goals into company strategy."

How to do that is captured in the SDG Compass according to the BSDC report's authors. Developed by the United Nations Global Compact, the World Business Council for Sustainable Development (WBCSD) and GRI, a pioneer of corporate sustainability reporting, the SDG Compass is a five-step guide for companies wishing to align their strategies with the SDGs. Backed up by a comprehensive website (www.sdgcompass.org) that includes tools and indicators the SDG Compass is a wonderful resource. But there is an issue.

On page 22 of the SDG Compass guide, under the title 'Anchoring sustainability goals within the business', the authors state:

> To be most effective, your company's sustainability goals should be an integral part of its full set of financial, strategic and operational goals, alongside goals for areas such as sales and productivity. Ultimately, the sustainability ambitions will also be reflected in the vision, mission and/ or purpose statements of the company, thereby fundamentally and prominently tying the company's future success to sustainable development.[2]

The key word here is "ultimately". To my mind reflecting the ambition of the company in its purpose is not the final but very the first step a business that is determined to change for good should be taking. And that is the key message of this book. Pursuing the adoption of, and attempting to embed, the SDGs, no matter how well intentioned, without first determining the core purpose of the business lays it open to all the sorts of challenges and accusations that perceived "bolt-on" CSR initiatives have attracted in the past.

What businesses really need in the first instance is an understandable, unifying, compelling, relevant and, yes, permanently sustainable conviction set right at the very heart of the business. A Single Organizing Idea (SOI) meets that criteria. In simple terms it's a strategic management tool that helps businesses revisit their *raison d'être* and then change at a practical pace from the core outward. It is what this book is about.

An SOI ties together the profit and social purpose of a business and makes it into an inspiring enterprise that multiple stakeholders can both contribute to and benefit from.

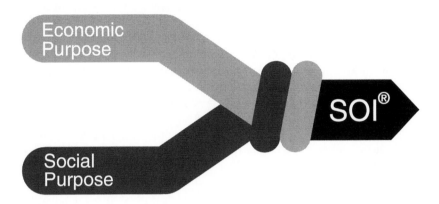

Figure 1 The power of a Single Organizing Idea

We begin with a story. It's completely fictitious but much of it is based on scenarios that we will all recognize and although the characters are purposefully larger than life stereotypes, they are based on real people I have come across. Brought together, their stories illustrate larger truths about the conflicts and challenges that are preventing businesses from changing and, on the opposite side, the forces that are driving and demanding change.

The second part of the book answers the question: "Why do businesses need to change?" Avoiding the usual clutch of overused case studies, it breaks out themes from the story and draws on real life examples and contemporary thinking to analyse in more detail the drivers that are rearranging the world we know. It concludes with descriptions of the many positive attributes of an SOI and its potential to tackle the drivers of change and turn challenges into opportunities.

The third and final part is a practical guide that will help leaders and practitioners in the field who want to know how to identify, define and implement an SOI. It is not a quick and easy process. It requires collaboration, commitment—particularly from senior managers and leaders—as well as patience and perseverance. It also requires a proven approach and in this part of the book I set out in detail the tools and methodologies I have adopted, refined and developed in a step by step way that draws on first-hand experience to help illustrate the real impact of change on a business.

At his home in London, Charles Handy—one of the world's most highly regarded business management thinkers—said to me "Your SOI has so much more potential to make a difference than a simple purpose". An SOI does indeed have value beyond purpose (see 'Ten things an SOI can do—and four it can't' on page 94 for the full list of benefits). While purpose articulates the potential the business may have to make a difference, having an SOI at the core of the business demonstrates the clear intent, and most importantly, the ability, to ensure purpose goes beyond words and is implemented. I don't pretend that an SOI provides a perfect answer and it is certainly not a "silver bullet". However, it can be applied in practice and it does work to change businesses into the sustainable, dynamic and socially connected entities that we now really need.

I'll conclude by saying that I'm not a sustainability expert or an academic with reams of research to draw on. I'm not a management guru and certainly not a visionary. I'm simply an experienced and knowledgeable practitioner who has had the privilege, over the last three decades, of drawing on the minds of many people from business, government, civil society and the media who've talked to me about their and our world. Lana Abu-Hijleh and a rainbow of others from across the planet have given me precious insights and invaluable opportunities to learn and understand. Their shared perspectives have refined my thinking, fired my passion for change, and ultimately led me to create this book. I hope you find it useful.

The thinking behind SOI is well developed, but that doesn't mean it shouldn't evolve and be improved, so I am keen to learn about others' successes and challenges and invite you to share your insights and experiences, either by contacting me via my email neil@neilgaught.com or through my website www.neilgaught.com/soi.html

Part 1

A change of fortune—
a story of our times

Introduction to part 1

What you are about to read is fiction. It's an entertaining short story that takes place across several continents, and contrasts a corporate catastrophe with the founding of a bright new enterprise. Nevertheless, as you will read, there is more than a grain of truth behind every word. So, please do read between the lines. For, whatever your response to this tale of misfortune and endeavour may be, herein lies a wake-up call for any business that wishes to change the nature of its fortune.

A change of fortune

Public Hearing: "The Cost of Heating"

European Parliamentary Committee on Industry, Research & Energy

József Antall Building, Brussels

Right now

With one comment, composed in haste and primed like a grenade, the chief executive of Europe's largest domestic energy supplier is seconds away from destroying everything he values in life.

"*Mr Halle, would you agree that the company policies you've outlined have placed customer lives at risk?*"

"No, Ma'am, I would not."

Glancing only briefly at his cell phone, while pretending to consult his briefing notes, Tomas Halle, Head of FuelGlow, finds the send button with his forefinger. He feels no need to check the line he's just dashed out. It's only a private message on Twitter, intended for one recipient only. Even with some typos, she'll understand why he hasn't been able to give it his full attention. Facing Tomas across the chamber, the committee chair peers over her glasses. She's been gunning for this showdown for months now. In the 20 minutes since the hearing opened, he's handled every question levelled at him without once leaving the script. Tomas congratulates himself for having personally appointed FuelGlow's Communications Director who sits one row back, and dispatches his message to her.

"*Then maybe we should explore the tragic case of Edith Benoit?*"

That name. The one name Tomas Halle had been assured he would not hear. He looks up with a start, his hand shrinking from the desk. Three men sit to his right, all of who have played this inquisition with the same pre-prepared statements. They're industry competitors, maybe, but just then this trio of energy bosses bristle like him.

"With respect," says Halle, "until the inquiry is complete I wouldn't wish to comment on –"

"With respect to Edith Benoit's family," the committee chair cuts in, and this time she waits until she has his full attention, "you really should be more forthcoming with your answers."

For six years now, Tomas Halle had steered FuelGlow with the calm authority of a captain on the bridge of a supertanker. In his experience, the waters could get a little choppy and nobody on board would notice. The key, he maintained, was in assembling a crew he could depend upon to manage such a massive vessel. Take the individual seated behind him, in what suddenly feels to Tomas like a gladiatorial amphitheatre. As soon as the committee summoned him to this hearing, prompted by what was frankly a provocative report linking a rise in hypothermia cases amongst the elderly with increased energy price rises, he had instructed her to deal with it. When it came to protecting the brand, Eve Grainger possessed the spin and bite of a black widow spider. "*We're seeking to stall the Benoit claim,*" she had told him only the week before over breakfast at the hotel where they liked to meet. "*It's a non-starter.*"

"Mr Halle, do I need to refresh your memory?"

The committee chair had leaned in to her microphone before pressing him once more. Not that she needed to make herself any clearer in the silence that seized the chamber. Despite his media training, with all the focus on symbolically grasping ownership of each question with his hands, Tomas instinctively reaches for his headset as if the translator has just caused him a problem.

"Exactly when did FuelGlow become aware that Madame Benoit was receiving treatment for clinical depression?" The chair continues. "What mechanisms do you have in place to safeguard the welfare of customers in her situation?"

Tomas Halle offers her a puzzled smile.

"We service millions of households," he says as if to remind her. "Not just one."

"Which is all the more reason to be sensitive to the impact of your behaviour as a company," she replies with no hint of amusement. "The fact is this poor woman felt so intimidated by the year on year rise in her fuel bill that she switched off her heating completely."

Tomas Halle senses his pulse points throbbing. He wants to tell her that nutters can be found in all walks of life, but is well aware of the sinkhole of grief that would open up for him. Halle might have found himself on the back foot with this question, but in need of some support from the figure sitting behind him, but he wasn't stupid. Only recently, in fact, FuelGlow's parent company had sent in some consultant to assess the company and report back to the president. Tomas had the guy's measure before they'd even shaken hands, and made it abundantly clear that he was in charge for good reason. Not that it really matters, he reminds himself briefly. Ever since the president turned his attention to developing world markets, Halle had been left to get on with what he did best: guaranteeing a return for the investor. There was no way he would let the actions of one muddled old lady undo his position now, or his share-price-linked bonus.

"We operate within industry guidelines," he tells the committee chair, wishing at the same time that Eve would hurry up and message him the response he so desperately needs. After the private joke he'd just sent, Halle expected her to come back at him straight away. It might've been in poor taste, concerning the warm temperature of the building and what it would take for her to cool off, but his phone just sits there uselessly. Much like Tomas at that moment. A line is all he needs from her right now. A response to steer the agenda back on his terms.

Across the chamber, with her eyes on the FuelGlow CEO still, the committee chair nods to herself.

"Indulge me for a moment, Mr Halle. Let's just say we were talking about your grandmother here –"

"*Oh, come on!*"

The voice from behind him, little more than an exasperated whisper, at least confirms to Tomas that Eve is still present. It's just enough to fire up a sense of indignation at the direction the chair has just taken.

"Ma'am, that's unkind."

"For a company that raised its domestic prices on the cusp of northern Europe's coldest winter in a decade," she continues, "I hardly think you're in a position to protest about unkindness. And that's what this all comes down to, Mr Halle. It's all very well to cite industry guidelines, and use them to justify obscene bonuses and salary increases, but when those guidelines put profit before humanity I feel a duty to take you to task."

Tomas Halle draws breath to respond, only to hold the thought he was set to express in case anger gets the better of him. Did he need to remind her that he was responsible for a multi-million dollar organization that was answerable to its shareholders? Yes, he had a duty of care to his customers, but that was based solely on the concept that they were able to pay! It was a simple business transaction. FuelGlow wasn't a charity, after all. The organization didn't exist to benefit society, though Tomas knew not to get into that argument and draw fire towards their tax practices. Even so, he thinks, this whole thing was so unnecessary. Did this woman with her high and mighty attitude have any idea how many people the company employed? Without FuelGlow, he thinks to himself, thousands of people would be without a salary, struggling to feed their families and keep them warm.

For this reason alone, Halle drops the argument from his mind.

As for the Benoit woman, well that was a tragedy, of course. A grieving widow slides into a fog of despair, and then cuts herself off from the world around including the power to heat her house. It was a damn shame, in Halle's view, but that didn't make the company wilfully complicit in her demise. If anything, the family that kicked up such a stink should take a long hard look at themselves. Where were they when Grandma stopped opening her curtains? For this reason, Eve had been quite correct in keeping Tomas out of the debate that followed. When a dead pensioner becomes the poster girl for an anti-fuel poverty movement, his role was to chart a steady course and have faith that the storm would weaken and fade.

What he hadn't banked on was the human iceberg currently refusing to break his gaze. Laura Valk, the Baltic Euro MP charged with chairing this hearing, belonged to some democratic green party Halle had never heard of before Eve briefed him. In her mid-fifties, he guessed, and with those glasses attached to a fine silver chain, Valk had offered him one brief smile when she formally opened the meeting. Even then, it had struck Tomas that she would be offering no further gesture of warmth. Mindful of his body language just then, Halle resists the urge to fold his arms.

"May I take this opportunity," he says after a moment, "to extend my sympathies to the family of Madam Benoit. "

"In what capacity?" asks Valk without even a blink. "Personally or as a company?"

"As a company," says Tomas, and glares right back at her, "we have *nothing* to apologise for." His response prompts a gasp from the public gallery. In his peripheral vision, Tomas notes several committee members confer, and yet this is between him and the chair now. "As a human being," he adds just to clarify, "of course I am sorry."

"If I may add something here." Seated beside Tomas, the CEO of The Charont Group speaks up in a way that sounds like a university professor addressing squabbling students. Tomas has respect for Anton van der Boor, but dislikes him intensely on a personal level. It wasn't just his trim figure, full head of silver hair or the fact that he outscores Halle on Glassdoor (Halle 25% CEO approval rate, van der Boor 38%). The guy just has this habit of making everyone around him feel inferior. On the upside, Tomas thinks, it takes the spotlight away from him. "It would be very easy to paint a picture of the energy industry as some kind of pantomime villain," continues van der Boor, "but let's not overlook our accomplishments in the field of corporate social responsibility. No doubt you'll be aware of the recent efforts made by Charont to encourage energy efficiency in the home. Our recent campaign saw just over 20% of our domestic customers install discounted smart meters."

Van der Boor looks around as if expecting a round of applause from the men flanking him. Halle wishes he'd been first to flag up their world-class CSR commitments. You just couldn't argue against a company that spent a bit of cash on the community, after all. Under the circumstances, however, he's quietly grateful to his business rival. Not only has Tomas forgotten the name of the guy who runs the CSR outfit, and whether it had been outsourced to Milan or Zurich, this intervention gives him a chance to check his phone. There's still no response from Eve to his direct message, though a mounting number of tweets await his attention when all this is over. Glancing up from his home screen, drawn by a muted cough from one of the committee members, he finds Laura Valk assessing them all.

"Gentlemen," she says eventually, "I don't wish to be drawn away from the reason why we've asked you before this committee."

"You can't just dismiss our good work in that field!" Van der Boor takes Halle by surprise with the force of his response. It's as if he's suddenly lost control of the irritation and annoyance that they all feel on being paraded here. Halle notes how he's just delivered his point by curling one hand into a particularly awkward looking thumb pointing fist. He hopes Eve is aware that he would never make such a basic error, and seizes the opportunity to regain control of the situation. When it comes to CSR, he thinks, his guys are leaders in the field.

"We provide a *free* domestic insulation assessment for all our customers," he begins. "Ultimately, FuelGlow aims to improve the lives of our customers."

"Apart from those who are scared of you!"

The outburst comes from the public gallery. It causes heads to turn. There, a young man is on his feet looking close to tears. At once, the security guard on the floor makes his way towards the gallery. Seeing him approach, the guy extends his palms to signal that his moment in the sun is done before dropping into his seat once more. Halle recognises the protestor. He's seen him on the TV, he thinks. A member of the Benoit family. Some nephew or a son-in-law. A troublemaker, for sure.

"I'm sorry," says the guy, gesturing toward Halle and the men beside him. "But you're letting these people get away with murder."

Tomas can feel his heart beating hard. This isn't how the hearing was supposed to shape up. In their briefing session, prior to coming here, Eve assured him that the answers she had prepared would see him through. He glances at the bullet points, noting her line about corporate social responsibility. That was the get out of jail card, as Eve had put it, only now that doesn't feel like such a certainty. With his pen in hand, Tomas Halle finds himself drawing a box around the line as if to set it apart from everything else. At the same time, his muted phone lights up to indicate an incoming message. Immediately, he sets the pen down, only to flatten his palm on the table and direct his full attention to the figure addressing them once more.

"If we can just return to the matter at hand," says Laura Valk, having taken a moment for everyone to settle down. "Setting aside all the creative ways you reduce your tax liability," she continues, which draws some amusement from her colleagues, "I want to understand your awareness of potential customer hardship when reviewing prices."

"It's complicated," replies van der Boor, like she wouldn't understand.

Valk sits back in her chair, removing her spectacles with one hand so they hang freely around her neck.

"Try me," she says, with a hint of relish.

All Tomas can do is focus on his body language, and reveal no hint of the fact that he's squirming on the inside. As van der Boor begins to outline the industry's revenue requirement calculations, he notes his phone screen light up once more to remind him of the waiting message. This time, feeling lost and close to panic, he presses the home button. It's with relief that he sees it's from Eve. She might be sitting in the row behind him, close enough to lean down and whisper in his ear, but since despatching that private joke to her Tomas has been feeling entirely adrift. His push notifications icon continues to tell him he's mentioned in a lot of public tweets. Nevertheless, his sole interest is in hearing from his Head of Communications.

With van der Boor purposely outlining every figure in the formula, Tomas Halle discretely opens the message. He scans the single line. It's a question, he registers—simple and to the point—but it's enough to trigger such a profound sense of dread that he looks up with a start.

What have you done?

*

FutureWorks Hybrid Seminar 4.0

African Union Conference Centre

Addis Ababa

Five minutes later

Bibi Okira passes through the security check with a sense of shared excitement. Having waited in line for some time, chatting to her fellow delegates, it's good to be inside such an impressive building. Looking up and around, she admires the combination of marble and vaulted glass. Outside, beyond the parade of national banners snapping in the breeze, Bibi looks out at the sprawl of buildings, trees and distant hills that define the Ethiopian capital. It's her first visit in eight years, and the commercial district has changed dramatically. Having flown in that morning from Kigali, she hopes to grab some time to explore before her flight home. For now, her attention is focused on the impending seminar. Having developed an app to bring together farmers with micro-investors, the young 'agri-preneur' is—like every delegate—here by invitation

Placing the lanyard around her neck, Bibi checks the information screen above the reception desk. Even before she locates the details, it's clear from the general direction of movement that the key plenary event is due to take place in the main hall. Joining the throng at the hall door, and knowing that her husband would be waiting to hear from her, she fishes out her phone to confirm her safe arrival. She smiles on finding a message from him, along with a clutch of work-related emails. She scrolls through quickly, scanning for a name she hopes to hear from at any time. With nothing yet, and people only filtering slowly through the hall, Bibi switches to her Twitter stream. Her intention is to see what other delegates are saying. Instead, as is often the way, her attention is drawn to a drama playing out in another part of the world.

"Oh dear," she says to herself, and promptly laughs out loud.

"*Care to share?*"

Bibi glances up to see a smartly dressed young man grinning broadly at her. He has a walkie-talkie in hand and a lapel badge sporting the conference logo.

"It's unrepeatable," she says, still chuckling, and pockets her phone. "But some people really need a license before using social media."

The young man hides a smile, on the cusp of laughing along with her if he wasn't there to steer the attendees, before inviting her to follow the crowd. As they gravitate towards the door, Bibi reflects on the story. Some old-school boardroom general unwittingly puts out a public tweet instead of a private message and effectively scuppers his career. She's heard of the company, too. It's one of Europe's energy giants. With the story climbing the global trending charts, what a nightmare in the making that must be, she thinks to herself, before finally entering the conference hall.

Inside, it takes a moment for Bibi's eyes to adjust. With the hall filling fast, she finds her seat and watches the technical crew make the final preparations for the forthcoming seminar. On the stage, spotlights shine on two chairs. In the background, a large screen sports the FutureWorks logo. The organization behind the conference has a reputation for hosting ground-breaking talks by business pioneers and game changers. Bibi considers her invite to be a privilege. Not only is it a chance to network with professionals who share her values and drive, the central speaker is an inspiration to her.

From her bag Bibi produces a notebook and pen. She also checks the time on her phone, as well as her email just in case the news she's anticipating has come in. Securing the right financial backer has been a priority for her lately. She's received several offers, but either their priorities or their values just didn't chime with her outlook and ambition. Yes, there was money to be made in facilitating business opportunities with farmers across Africa, but her commitment to empowering their position shone just as brightly. With a couple of minutes to go, and nothing new in her inbox, the young entrepreneur can't resist checking her Twitter feed one more time. Sure enough, the chatter surrounding the power chief's indiscretion continues to grow. Not only are the retweets accompanied by barbed comments, people are starting to post TV stills showing the hapless boss at the hearing. Some feature jokey text at his expense overlaid across it. "*When I get cold I burn £20 notes*" says one, while another declares "*early retirement never looked so attractive*". She feels torn. On the one hand, it's enormously entertaining. On the other, now she reads up on the background to this story, people's lives have come to depend on giants of industry such as this.

Frankly, thinks Bibi Okira as a round of applause greets the appearance on stage of the MC, they deserve better.

*

At the first opportunity, as the chair rounds on the quietest of the big four energy chiefs, Tomas Halle deletes the offending tweet.

At a glance, this one off-the-cuff quip, intended as a private communication with a trusted colleague, has been shared thousands of times. Halle feels sick to his stomach as he refreshes his feed to confirm it has gone, and then powers down his phone for good measure. He doesn't use social media very much. In fact, it was Eve who set up his account so he could share press releases or make industry-related comments that she wrote in his name. It was all good public-facing stuff, she told him. Makes you look approachable. Open. Caring. In-touch. Lately, they'd used the direct message function to communicate off the record, which is something the CEO of FuelGlow now bitterly regrets. He just hopes that with the tweet removed people will move on.

"*So, would you agree with that assertion, Mr Halle? What is your analysis?*"

"I'm sorry. What was that?"

Tomas lifts his gaze across the chamber. The chair, Laura Valk, is peering over the top of her glasses at him once more.

"Mr. Halle, do you need a break? You look a little pale."

"Ma'am, I welcome this debate. I simply missed the point you just made."

Tomas cringes inwardly, and instructs himself to focus hard. Yes, he might've just caused a small fuss online, but that could happen to anyone. With several industry journalists in the press gallery, it was his performance here that mattered most. Having positioned his body language to convey calm control over the situation, despite feeling so rattled, Halle listens to Valk repeat herself for his benefit.

"I recognise the undertaking involved in delivering your services is significant," she tells him, "but I'm just not convinced it justifies your position that nothing can be done to improve things. The fact is you've just shrugged your shoulders at every criticism raised here, cited statistics and shifted attention towards your corporate social work." Valk pauses there as if seeking the right expression. "It just feels so... superficial. It's an exercise in greenwashing, no? Forgive me for being blunt, Mr Halle, but I see a distinct lack of will to *genuinely* make a difference. Surely companies of your size and importance must share a desire to be regarded by society as a positive force?"

Halle doesn't need to consult his fellow bosses to know they share the same sentiment as him. He can practically hear each of them blow the air from their cheeks in exasperation.

"I believe we need to manage expectation here," he says, which is about as polite a way as he can put it. Asking an energy giant to step up and save the world was both fanciful and impossible. From the bridge of his supertanker, you didn't just issue the order to spin around and steam off in search of some mythical land. It had taken decades to establish momentum. Everyone knew the course ahead and those who had fuelled the journey expected reward for their commitment. Yet again, that was business. Something this green-blooded Eurocrat failed to fully grasp. "I'm sure that politicians strive to be regarded as a positive force in just the same way," Tomas adds with a chuckle, and is delighted when a ripple of amusement spreads out across the chamber.

Only Valk fails to crack a smile.

By now, it strikes Tomas Halle that the chair has undermined her position by expressing such a level of idealism. Her misgivings about their corporate social endeavours also suggested to him that she didn't really understand the game.

Halle himself had been late to sign up to the reputational capital to be gained from such side interests. Under his watch, however, FuelGlow had established an entire department dedicated to investing in high profile community projects. Their work served the press office, feeding them with material for dazzling media releases, which justified their existence as far as he was concerned. Tomas even goes so far as to read out the list prepared for him. It sounds like the work of a corporate saint in his opinion, and yet Valk remains unimpressed. This is evident in the way she removes her glasses just then—as if to address the energy chiefs on a different level.

"I'm not here to pass judgement," she says, upon which Tomas just about holds back a splutter. "For now, my role is to determine the facts. And whatever the outcome from this hearing, gentlemen, you can be assured that the customer will make informed decisions. But speaking on a personal level, and not as the committee chair," she continues, "I would like to think that my energy supplier was driven by the needs of society as much as the desire to turn a profit. An organization that shows as much sensitivity to the consumer and the environment as it does to its shareholders."

By now, Tomas Halle is so incensed by Valk's unrealistic attitude that he opts to say nothing for a moment. Behind him, he can hear Eve tapping away on her phone. Apart from one less than helpful message, she has singularly failed to provide him with any further assistance in dealing with this troublemaker. That he's had his phone switched off for a little while now is irrelevant. If he's on his own here, Tomas thinks to himself, then so be it.

"As a company we constantly strive to improve," he begins.

"As an *industry*," the figure beside him cuts in, which causes Halle to release his intake of breathe with a sigh, "it is our duty to work towards the standards you've just set out."

Van der Boor's intervention brings silence to the chamber. Halle notes him settle back in his seat, one forearm resting casually across the table in a manner that Eve would never allow. Unwilling to allow his rival to steal the moment, Tomas Halle leans forward to command the chair's attention once more.

"It's a question of leveraging our core competency," he says, quite certain that a phrase Halle himself only picked up in recent weeks won't have appeared on the committee chair's radar. He allows himself a small smile, but it only serves to harden Valk's expression.

"Your sound-bites really do roll off the tongue." Valk restores her spectacles to the mid-section of her nose once more. On instinct, Tomas Halle glances across at his neighbour. He finds van der Boor doing exactly the same thing to him. "but regardless of the jargon if you're genuinely in agreement with me," she continues, "then surely we're talking about something deeper? Let's face it, the fact that you're being forced to defend your reputation here, rather than allowing it to speak for itself, must tell you something is very wrong. Right now, the general public see you as a faceless moneymaking machine that allows pensioners to freeze for the sake of profit. That might seem harsh, but it's also not sustainable for you as a business model. Something has to give here if you're going to restore public confidence."

Tomas Halle considers what Valk has just said; a little shocked by her intensity, and comes to just one conclusion. She's gunning for his resignation. And that isn't going to happen in the face of what has become borderline hysteria. Halle wasn't aware of the Benoit case for a while. At least, not until that pointedly provocative article tried to pin her death on FuelGlow. It was pure mischief making, as he'd said at the time, and he sure as hell wasn't going to be held personally responsible now. With so many other factors involved, his sole duty was to prevent FuelGlow from being steered off course. The company had clear goals, as the shareholders expected to see in each quarterly results, and it fell to him to keep things nice and steady. With his gaze on Valk, Tomas Halle leans into his microphone as if to address her alone.

"Perhaps you could share your solution," he says, and tips his head to feign interest.

For a moment, Laura Valk just blinks at him. It's as if he's just called her out for basing her whole argument on a nice idea. Then she spreads her hands as if appealing to the chamber for a sense of reason.

"Mr Halle, I'm suggesting there needs to be a fundamental change in the purpose of your existence," she says finally. "Ultimately, there must be a better means of doing business. There just has to be for all our sakes. And if you understood the benefits, I have no doubt you'd find a way."

The FutureWorks compere is as relaxed in front of his audience as he is for the weekly current affairs debate show he hosts on television. Dressed in jeans, a collarless shirt and canvas jacket, with sandy hair and an easy smile, Dan Caplin is quick to engage with his audience and share his enthusiasm for the forthcoming event. Bibi has just watched him welcome a familiar face onto the stage. As Caplin says himself, it's an honour to see her here. A Canadian author, social activist and documentary maker, Nell Stevens is instantly recognisable by the striking grey streak that runs through her long black hair. She settles in her chair with a copy of her latest bestseller in her lap; a book Caplin described as "proving that in the right hands capitalism and caring can share a lot more than the same first letter." Now, he's turned his attention to the big screen behind them, which is host to a logo that has become as familiar to Bibi as Apple and Coca Cola.

"Twelve years ago, when he took over the reins of a long-running, but arguably little-known knitwear company, nobody had any idea of the transformation that he was about to implement. Had I known", Dan continues, facing the front once more to address the hall through his headset, "I'd have camped outside his office door until he hired me. I'm talking about a man who took a tired, old-fashioned American manufacturing business, reliant on a shrinking well of ageing customers, and transformed it into the most profitable social enterprise on the planet. This is an individual who fiercely believes that it's possible to combine idealism with a practical outlook that results in both profit and purpose, he expanded and diversified his interests internationally; entering markets where the buzz about his approach created opportunities for all. As I'm sure you know, his organization's year-on-year growth rate has been remarkable. In a moment from now, we'll hear from the figurehead behind it all. A man who passionately believes in engaging closely with communities worldwide, whose focus and vision is said to instigate positive and lasting change, and effectively showcases the rewards that come from a single-minded and ruthless determination to ignore the cynics and compete through the pursuit of a profit and social purpose agenda." Caplin stops there, steps aside and raises one hand towards the screen. "Ladies and gentlemen. Live from his headquarters in Los Angeles, it gives me great pleasure to welcome the head of Soul House, *Conrad James!*"

Like everyone seated around her, clapping enthusiastically now, Bibi's attention switches to the screen. There, a video feed replaces the logo. It reveals a figure framed by an ocean view from the bay window behind him. Conrad James is seated at a desk space with just a laptop to one side and a pitcher of water with a glass beside it. He's trim, tanned, wearing a white shirt open at the throat, and smiling broadly at the audience. Bibi can't help pay attention to the view from his office. Breakers can be seen rolling in from the Pacific; framed by spear-leaved plants on the headland. How blessed must he feel, she wonders, to be rewarded on so many levels?

"Thank you, Dan, for that introduction," says Conrad, speaking in a light Midwest accent. "Rest assured the next job vacancy is yours."

The audience laughs, as does the compare and his stage guest.

"You know, I have one question I've always wanted to ask you." Caplin takes his seat beside Nell Stevens as he speaks. "We often read articles and papers that analyses your work, but this is an opportunity to hear from you first hand."

"Shoot," says Conrad, listening with interest.

"You're an entrepreneur who started out in knitwear, but your organization has gone way beyond that now."

"From fibres and yarn to medicine distribution," says Conrad, cutting in with a smile. "I know where this is heading."

"Then this is your chance to enlighten us," says Caplin, addressing the audience as much as the man on the video feed. "Your portfolio is so diverse it could easily become a mess. Exactly how do you make it work together?"

As James considers the question, Bibi studies his face and hopes that one day people might ask her the same thing.

"My business interests might seem eclectic," he begins, "but every single one shares the same common purpose, and that's to ensure that what is good for business is good for the planet and us lot inhabiting it."

"Which is easy to say," replies Caplin, clearly having anticipated the answer. "But in reality surely money talks?"

Nell Stevens swings her attention back to the screen. Caplin has come straight to the point here, and it's clear she's interested in seeing how he handles it.

"Money speaks as loudly today as it always has," agrees the Soul House chief. "But the world in which we live has changed dramatically in the space of a decade. Today, people want to be assured that with success we're also behaving responsibly in the marketplace, and I think we all recognise how technology has driven that. Just look at us, conversing live across continents as if we're in the same room. That would've been unthinkable until recently, and now we take it for granted. So, we're connected, 24 hours a day, and that's had a monumental influence on the way we do business."

"My wife makes me switch my phone to silent at night," Caplin interjects, which draws more laughter from the hall. "For me, business stops at bedtime."

"She's a wise woman," chuckles Conrad, "but that just goes to show what an impact this has had on us, and not just as individuals. As businesses," he continues, and meshes his fingers together, "we're more connected with our customers than ever before. Of course, through advertising and PR we've been speaking to *them* for decades, but thanks to social media that one-way flow of communication has become a conversation... and more importantly people talk to each other."

"We can't just sell them a line," says Nell Stevens, nodding at the same time.

"Exactly." Conrad tips his head to register her point. "The public are well aware of the power in their hands, and demand that companies operate responsibly. It means the days of spin are over," he says. "If you tell the customer one thing, but you're doing another, they'll know. And when they find out they'll share that information and there's nothing you can do about it. Nothing at all."

As Conrad reaches for his glass of water just then, Bibi uses the opportunity to check she's muted her phone.

"In a sense you paint a surprisingly bleak picture," says Caplin, which prompts Conrad to set down his glass.

"On the contrary, I consider it to be a liberation! In this age of transparency, it means we're forced to operate with nothing to hide. Companies can't just conjure up some CSR venture and hope that keeps everyone sweet. Granted, some projects might make a difference, but they're never undertaken as part of the core business. It's ad hoc and unsustainable. Something a company does because they feel they have to. Only now, when their behaviour suggests other motives, it makes them look even worse! And the real tragedy here is that we live in a world that desperately needs business to get behind social change. What I'm suggesting is that there's a relationship to be had with mutual benefit."

"But just how do we bring them together?" asks Caplin.

"At the end of the day, we're human beings," Conrad continues. "We want to be recognised for our positive qualities, and the drive for profit and purpose enables us to achieve just that. I'm lucky, in many ways. I no longer have to scramble for short-term profit to please my shareholders. Right from the beginning, I made it very clear that I wasn't looking for backers interested in making a fast buck. What's interesting is that smart investors know how badly that plays in this day and age. Yes, it requires commitment, but those who came on board could see the long-term benefit. They're as committed as I am to steady, sustainable growth."

"And when you say growth," says Nell with a hint of mischief, "does that also mean profit?"

"Of course!" Conrad doesn't hesitate in responding. "There's no shame in making money with this approach to business. It demands it, in fact. Because money makes the world go round, right? If we're ever going to sort out the world's problems, if we are ever going to achieve those 17 Sustainable Development Goals the world signed up to we need to be able to pay for it. This is precisely how and where businesses that have social purpose at their core can help."

Bibi drinks in the words of her hero. It was Conrad's book that she had read two years earlier that had moved her to do something in the first place. As a former outreach worker, working within rural Rwandan communities, she had recognised the frustrations experienced by small agricultural ventures in connecting with the right investor. Often, the physical distance between the two parties was a barrier. Not only did Bibi realise how a smartphone app could help bring them together, and set about devising software that enabled the value created by her venture to be shared, she recognised that it had the potential to maintain and grow a sustainable partnership. Now here she was, awaiting news that could see her dream come true. And yes, she thought, as Dan Caplin invites Nell to raise a point. Her reputation was in its infancy, but that had got her the attention of the right backer and she was proud of it.

"As you know," begins Nell, addressing the man on the screen, "I'm broadly supportive of your aims and objectives. But I wonder how much of this is about a more sophisticated form of reputation or formal management? The drive for authenticity can only be encouraged. But it has to come from the heart, no? You can take years to establish your business, only to see your reputation collapse in a click."

Caplin shares a flutter of laughter from the audience. He squints into the stage light, nodding at the same time.

"I think some of us are keenly aware of an example unravelling in real time right now."

"The FuelGlow fiasco?" this is Conrad, who doesn't share Caplin's sense of glee but clearly recognises the implications. "That goes to show how one slip has the potential to ruin a man as much as a business. What's more, as a result of that poor guy's personal indiscretion, the *world* is now watching an obscure committee hearing as it takes apart Europe's energy titans. As we speak, they're being found out."

"Some might say that's a good thing," suggests Nell.

"In a strange way, I regard it as cathartic," replies Conrad, nodding. "The digital revolution fuelling how we communicate is catching out the old guard. It can be catastrophic for them, as I believe we're seeing today, but it also forces a change for the better. If we can get people like you guys over there in that room to come on board with the basic principle of business that has purpose then I genuinely believe the collective spirit of us all will propel the way we do things forward. It'll help us to build a better world for all, and crucially, allows us to make money. Profit is the lifeblood of any business, after all, but it doesn't have to be toxic."

"That's all well and good," says Nell, cutting straight back at Conrad, "but what are the tools for making that happen?" She glances at the audience, and offers them a conspiratorial smile. "I really think we need to understand more about how you make it happen."

Nell's intervention causes the atmosphere in the hall to tighten. Bibi smiles to herself. As much as she admires Conrad James, it's good to see someone prepared to hold his feet to the fire. Conrad himself takes the question with an air of openness and grace.

"If you asked me how it affects the bottom line, we wouldn't just look at the figures but the *emotional* impact," he says, "and for some that's hard to comprehend. But the fact is it can make the difference between failure and success, and if you can grasp the reason why then we're half way there. Do you feel good about what you're doing, for example, and how about your staff, customers and the wider community? Ultimately, do they respect the way you behave and value your goods and services? It all feeds in, and critically serves as the engine for success."

"So, start her up," says Nell with a smile, which only endears her to the audience. Like Bibi, it's clear she wants to focus on the practical process behind his business outlook. "Let's hear how she sounds and judge that for ourselves."

"OK." Conrad is smiling, enjoying the exchange. "First and foremost, you need to be prepared to open up and examine the very heart of your business. You need to identify the purpose of its existence. It might be something you've yet to define, or perhaps it's become buried over time. If you take the right approach you will not only uncover the purpose of your business but the Single Organizing Idea that will put it at your core and help you align with it."

Throughout, Nell faces the audience as if asking everyone to consider how this applies to them.

"Perhaps you can take Soul House as an example," says Dan. "Take us through the process that helped you find the hidden purpose and Single Organizing Idea that catapulted that knitwear business all those years ago."

As Conrad James returns to his days working from a rented space in downtown Phoenix, Bibi finds she's listening with an eager spirit. So far, everything Conrad has shared chimes with her way of thinking and helps to crystallise her faith in his approach and the thoughts she has about her fledgling business. Listening intently, she pops the lid of her pen again, circles S.O.I. and smiles inside.

*

Tomas Halle straightens his notes and caps his pen in a slow, deliberate fashion. After that car crash of a hearing, he has no intention of rising to leave just yet. That would invite eye contact with people he was in no mood to see right now, which amounted to pretty much everyone in the chamber.

"We need to get you out of here."

The FuelGlow CEO can't even bring himself to glance over his shoulder to acknowledge Eve. He's just come through the worst hour of his life. A grilling that could've been handled so much better had he not relied on a bunch of bullet points that proved to be way off target. He doesn't even want to think about the embarrassment he's caused himself on social media. Having shut down his phone, he's in no hurry to fire it back up. What he doesn't know, he tells himself, can't hurt him. Maybe later, he decides, he'll creep back on and delete his whole account.

"That went well," says the figure on his feet beside him.

Tomas glances up to see van der Boor looking hunted and pale. If he'd just been ironic with Halle, his Dutch accent disguised it. Nevertheless, there's no hiding the fact that he's perspiring at the temples, and clearly in need of loosening his tie. Despite it all, Halle takes some pleasure in seeing the man no longer look as if he's born to rule.

"We all have bad days," Tomas replies "It'll blow over."

"I'm not so sure." Van der Boor says this with his gaze fixed across the chamber. There, the woman responsible for making them squirm is filing her way out. She's chatting with one of her colleagues. They could be talking about how their children are faring at school, Halle thinks bitterly. As if perhaps sensing their focus on her, Laura Valk glances across at the two men. She pauses for a moment, clutching a folder to her chest, before offering them both a smile. There's nothing provocative or gleeful about it, however. If anything, notes Halle, it's the sort of look you might receive if you've just experienced bereavement. It's enough to spark some anger in him, which he expresses by scooping up his notes and his phone and then dumping them inside his briefcase.

"We'll get through this," he tells his fellow CEO. "All storms die out. They always do."

A hand clasps his elbow just then. Tomas looks around to find his Head of Communications wearing such an expression of anxiety he almost fails to recognise her.

"I'm trying to secure us a side exit but I don't think security will allow it."

Instead of the warrior princess, as Halle once so fondly described her, Eve Granger looks like she's just learned that the oxygen is about to run out in the building. She's visibly rattled. Clutching her phone and with her bag slung over one shoulder, she tugs on his elbow once more. "Let's try not to make any further comments on the way out shall we?"

"Because of this?" For a chief executive who has just been left unable to provide an answer to the chair's ultimate question, Tomas Halle finds his sense of defeat turn to indignation. Did Valk seriously expect him to come up with an instant solution to an age-old issue? The energy sector was a messy business. From the process of extracting oil and gas from the ground to the delivery of the end product, some people would always be unhappy. His role was to make sure FuelGlow complied, minimised risk, and didn't get side-tracked into seeking a cure for cancer or some such. Even now, after such a roasting, anyone who thought otherwise needed to face a hall full of shareholders. Then let's see how they felt about single-handedly saving the world. Eve's grip tightens on Halle's elbow just then, drawing him from his thoughts. He shrugs her off, making way for van der Boor at the same time, who leaves with his entourage. "This whole hearing has been a stitch up."

"It's not been good," she agrees, before her gaze falls to the ground between them. "But it looks worse online," she adds in a small voice.

"That tweet was a mistake." Halle gathers his case; keen to get away now so he can express himself a little more openly. "I got rid of it straight away."

Eve meets his gaze once more, and it's searching.

"You're needed back at the office," she says simply. "Halodi have been calling. Mr Tang himself wants to speak to you."

Halle had just moved to follow van der Boor, but this news causes him to falter in his step. Based in Singapore, Halodi Holdings Inc. held majority shares in FuelGlow. Halle had always enjoyed a comfortable relationship with the conglomerate. They respected his experience and simply let him continue to keep the supertanker on course. Lately, however, ever since a boardroom reshuffle that saw Su Lien Tang in the big seat, he had found the nature of their relationship changing. In a sense, with Tang's enthusiasm for ventures with social and financial capital, the FuelGlow CEO had sensed the spotlight shift away from his company. Tang still checked in with him on a regular basis, but more often than not Halle would find himself nodding along as the guy talked up some pet project in a market that was far outside his experience or interest. And what of the consultant that Halodi had embedded with him recently? Halle considered it to be no more than a gesture to remind him that he wasn't entirely free to do as he pleased, and that was fine by him. What mattered, as he always maintained, was the return he delivered.

"But my conference call with Mr Tang is always scheduled for the end of the week," he tells Eve quietly, well aware that people are registering his presence as they head towards the chamber doors. "Can't it wait?"

Eve slows for the bottleneck at the exit. She turns, her lips pressed flat, and shakes her head.

"It can't wait," she says. "I'm sorry."

＊

Via video link, from his offices in California, Conrad James seeks to play down the applause from the African Union Conference Centre hall. Dan Caplin, the seminar facilitator, is on his feet; his clapping amplified a touch by the microphone attached to his headset.

"Thank you, sir, on behalf of everyone here, for what proved to be a deeply enlightening and inspiring session."

"It's been my pleasure," says Conrad. "I feel it's a great privilege to share my thinking and for it to be received with such enthusiasm. But this really isn't about me," he adds. "I'm part of a movement, and it's growing every day."

"I believe even Nell might be heartened to hear that." Caplin steps to one side to draw attention to his guest who shares the stage, "and that really is saying something."

Nell laughs, as does the audience. From where Bibi Akira is sitting, it's been a good-natured but rigorous conversation, and Nell's questions have certainly kept the Soul House founder focused. She looks at her notes, underlining the trinity of letters that stand out among all the observations she's taken down the power and potential of a Single Organizing Idea strikes her again.

"I sense we're all on the same page," says Conrad just then. "Writing in different styles, perhaps, but telling the same story and wanting the same outcome."

"Well, it's been a pleasure to hear your insights."

Dan Caplin takes a step back, extending his hand towards the screen at the same time.

"It's been a blast, Conrad. I wish you and Soul House, all the very best for the future."

"Likewise," says Conrad, and finds the camera lens in such a way that Bibi thinks he could be addressing her directly. "If I can leave you with one thing, it's this: Whatever you choose to do, in life as in business, your reputation will always precede you. That shouldn't make it your guiding force," he cautions, and raises his index finger. "All that matters is what you're doing to earn it in the first place."

Another round of applause fills the hall, for Dan and Nell as much as Conrad, before the screen returns to the Soul House logo. Bibi Okira gathers her bag as the house lights fade up. Chatter fills the air as people begin to file from the hall. She's tired, having travelled so far to get here, but deeply enthused.

On her way out, the young entrepreneur retrieves her phone from her bag and switches it off silent. Outside the building she takes herself to one side in order to make a phone call. Many people in attendance are here as business colleagues, and clearly have much to discuss. In the same way, Bibi is keen to share what she's learned with her husband. He's supported her this far, and knows how much she's been looking forward to this seminar. The light is intense, forcing her to turn away from the sun to see the screen. It's then Bibi notes the missed call. Registering the international number, the one she's been expecting all this time, she hurriedly engages the new message and presses the phone to her ear.

Standing on the lawn before the African Union Conference Centre, under the parade of flags that make up all the countries of the continent, Bibi Akira focuses hard as the message plays out. She closes her eyes, having devoted herself to working towards this moment for some time now. A second later, all the tension in her bearing drops away. She breaks into a heartfelt smile, and curls her free hand into a fist. A moment later, she hurriedly dials home.

"It's me," she tells her husband, grinning at the carefully clipped grass. "Yes, yes, it was amazing. I have so much to tell you, but listen," she says, and her face lights up once again. "I have news… the call came through from Halodi. And they want to invest in me!"

*

Tomas Halle flops into the taxi and orders the driver to take them on the short ride to the FuelGlow building. That's not so easy, given the startling number of journalists and photographers flocking around the vehicle.

"What just happened?" he asks, still reeling from the flashbulbs. Having stepped out into a media scrum, with the focus entirely on him, Halle takes a second to catch his breath. Beside him, Eve Grainger looks equally shocked.

"This could've been avoided," she says, and attempts to shield her face from the camera lens thrust against the window.

As the taxi finds space, much to Halle's relief, he leans forward and rests his head in his hands.

"I can't believe you failed to brief me properly," he mutters. "You hung me out to dry back there!"

"You did that to yourself."

Tomas hears his Head of Communications clearly. He just can't quite believe her attitude. He turns to look at her side on.

"Shall we talk about your briefing notes?" he asks pointedly.

"No." Eve answers with a level of defiance in her voice that once convinced Tomas that she was up to the task of protecting him as much as the brand. "Let's talk about a message you shared with the whole world back there!"

"That?" Tomas is genuinely surprised that Eve should be so concerned about such a trivial detail. He reaches for the roof strap as the taxi turns at a junction. "OK, so I made a mistake. I deleted the tweet as soon as I realised, but nothing is going to change how I just got chewed up back there!"

"We're finished," says Eve, facing forward once more.

Tomas takes a moment to consider this.

"Do you mean us?" he asks.

"I mean you, I mean me, I mean possibly the whole business. Tomas, you might consider one slip up on social media to be insignificant, but people took an interest and it brought that hearing to the attention of millions!"

"So, we're back to the briefing notes again," he mutters.

"*Forget the briefing notes!*" The force of Eve's response surprises Tomas. He turns to see her looking equally shocked, as if her outburst had just happened before she could stop herself.

"OK, let's calm down here." Instinctively, Tomas seeks to regain control of the situation. "We'll get back to the office and work out a press release."

Much to his surprise, Eve recovers her composure to respond with a small chuckle. Then, as the taxi approaches the company headquarters, she rests her head back and laughs. It would be funny were it not be such an expression of despair.

"I'm sorry," she says eventually, in a way that leaves Tomas wondering what she's apologising for. A moment later, the cab pulls up outside the building. Eve grasps the door handle before the automatic safety lock disarms. "OK," she says when it finally releases. "I'm out of here."

Before he can draw breath, Eve has stepped out onto the pavement. She leaves the cab door open, turns her back on Tomas and walks away.

With a sigh, the FuelGlow CEO pays the cab driver and reminds himself that in a moment from now he'll be safely inside his office. Back at the helm of the supertanker...

"Mr Halle, you have a video conference call waiting. Mr Tang is on hold."

As Tomas steps out of the lift, his secretary looks up and actually rises to her feet. Having had a moment to gather his composure, he strides across the floor doing his level best to portray a man going about his business as usual. Even so, his first impression is of a workplace in some state of meltdown. Phones are ringing at every station, while the conversations that meet his ears sound frantic and frayed at the edges. Several people register his arrival, stop what they're doing and stare.

"I'll take it right now," he says, passing the reception desk with his gaze fixed on his office. "Let's get this done."

Closing the door behind him, facing his expansive desk, Tomas Halle drops his case and lets his shoulders sink. In shock still from his reception outside the hearing, and with a dawning realisation that the whole situation has spiralled out of his control, he feels sick to his core. In the back of his mind, and he doesn't want to think about it now, his wife and family will no doubt have questions for him. His gaze switches to his computer screen. Somewhere behind the after dinner speech he'd been working on earlier, a videoconference window awaits him. With no time to think of a way out of this, and having witnessed his communications director desert him, Halle takes to his chair and reaches for the mouse.

"Mr Tang," he says, forcing himself to sound cheerful as Halodi's President appears on the screen. Su Lien Tang might be based in Singapore, but just then it feels like he's right here in Halle's office, and there's no escape. For a moment the man in the neat suit and glasses simply stares at Tomas.

"I tried to reach your cell phone," he says finally. "But it goes straight to answer machine."

"It's switched off." Halle laughs nervously. "I had some online trouble and needed to focus on the matter at hand."

Tang considers him for what feels like an age.

"I think you know why I've been trying to reach you so urgently, Tomas."

"Look," says Halle, and holds up his hands. "I know it didn't go well, but we're hardly talking about an oil spill here."

"On the contrary," says Tang, addressing him with impeccable pronunciation for a man speaking a second language. "The consequences of your actions have caused immeasurable damage. Not only have you bought FuelGlow into disrepute, your performance today served to highlight what a dinosaur you have allowed the organization to become. Throughout that hearing," he presses on, cutting across Halle as he draws breath to defend himself, "you repeatedly failed to give an honest answer, and do you know why? *Because the truth about the behaviour of the company is as shameful as your personal conduct!*"

"Sir, that's harsh."

"And undeniable!" By now Su Lien Tang's displeasure is in full effect. There is thunder in his expression as he speaks, which just leaves Halle feeling ill. "I learned a great deal from watching your performance," he continues, calming slightly, but not enough for Halle to relax. "For some time now, I've been undertaking a comprehensive review of Halodi's interests. In effect, I want to sleep at night, and feel that all our interests are making a positive contribution."

"Sir, we have an admirable record in the field of corporate respons-"

Halle stops there, silenced by a hand raised to the camera.

"We can't continue like this. There's no future for companies unable to operate with complete transparency."

"Impossible," says Halle. "There will always be aspects of our industry that just don't sit well with the consumer."

"In its current form, you're absolutely right," nods Tang, "which is why we need to take a long, hard look at ourselves and fundamentally change our approach. We need a new sense of direction, Mr Halle, "with long-term objectives in place of short-term results."

"But the quarterly reports," reasons Tomas, who has marked out his entire career by dividing each year into four. "The shareholders…"

"Are under review," says Tang, which is enough to silence Halle. "Speaking frankly," he continues, "it's time we behaved more like a social enterprise. One with both profit and purpose at its core. In fact, just today I've authorised significant impact investment in an agricultural development venture in Rwanda. No doubt you'd dismiss it as an act of charity, but that would be to fundamentally misunderstand their aims and intentions. We expect to see a return, Mr Halle, not just financially but in terms of tangibly improving lives. That's exactly the kind of partnership driving Halodi now. In many ways, it's a question of bringing together the best of the commercial and NGO sectors to create something greater than the sum of its parts. I see it as a natural evolution, in fact, and FuelGlow can be part of this process."

"It can?" Tomas makes no effort to hide his surprise. He grips the edge of his desk, as if perhaps letting go might lead to him toppling backwards.

"We might be talking about very different sectors," continues Tang, "but the driving force is just the same."

"Good." Tomas likes the sound of this, and begins to nod enthusiastically. "Where do we start?"

"With a change of leadership." Tang doesn't even blink when he says this. "Until today, Mr Halle, I had been minded to disregard my consultant's assessment of your position. You've been a loyal servant, after all."

"I bring in results," says Halle, unable to hide his irritation.

"You do indeed." Tang pauses there. "But the fact is we just don't share a common purpose any longer. Now, I have no doubt that given the opportunity you'd sit there and promise me change is in hand, but frankly that change has to come from the heart. And judging by your performance today, Mr Halle, it's clear your heart is just not in it."

Even before Tang sits back in his chair, the soon-to-be ex-CEO has dropped his gaze from the screen. He stares at his desk, in shock and dismay, but doesn't protest or plead for a second chance. If anything, he can be sure of just one thing. After everything he's just learned from this day, and in the face of all that he's lost, Tomas Halle recognises that Tang is making exactly the right move.

Part 2

The case for change

Introduction to part 2

They say that fact follows fiction. When I first sat down with Matt Whyman (my story-writing partner), my aim was to create a global stage upon which our larger-than-life archetypes could play out their roles as winners and losers in a fast-changing world.

The story that we plotted out together that day—across a hotel breakfast table with sugar cubes and miniature pots of jam—is based on real people I've met along the way and actual events. But I purposefully mixed them up so that we could freely explore the conflict of agendas, opportunities and challenges that our new hyper-connected planet presents.

That said, I had no idea just how close to the truth our final story was until I did some follow-up fact checking. In March 2016 *Panorama*, the BBC's current affairs flagship, aired a programme entitled 'Too Poor to Stay Warm.' Over thirty minutes the show's presenter, investigative journalist Datshiane Navanayagam, discusses a shocking set of facts with a range of people from energy consumers to energy company representatives, activists, experts and academics. According to Dr Jessica Allen of University College London, 9,000, mainly elderly citizens, died in 2015 in the UK as a result of not being able to keep warm in their own homes. That's in the world's fifth largest economy.*

"Fuel poverty", as it's termed, affects a staggering five million people in the UK and research shows that 12 million British citizens are regularly skipping meals in order to pay their energy bills. The facts are shocking but it's the back-story about the quasi-autonomous bodies that influence energy policy and the corporate government relationships that I found particularly interesting. Panorama not only shone a flashlight on the growing divide between rich and poor, it highlighted the consequences of a fiercely competitive and complex world where the pursuit of profit brings wealth to a few and daily misery to many.

---

* Latest World Bank data, 2015.

Six months later, on September 20th the pursuit of profit could not have been any more dramatically brought to life than when US Senator Elizabeth Warren didn't just bring a flashlight but a surgical knife to a Banking Committee Hearing. In an extraordinary tirade, Senator Warren started a 15-minute destruction of Wells Fargo's hapless CEO John Stumpf by quoting from his firm's vision and values statement "...if you want to find out how strong a company's ethics are don't listen to what its people say, watch what they do." "So" she added "let's do that." What followed was what the *Washington Post* described as a "brutal pummelling" during which the Senator repeatedly asked the CEO to resign and give back money he took while an alleged scam was going on.* In a tweet posted after the hearing, Senator Warren fired a final shot, "A bank cashier who steals $20 would be facing theft charges, but Wall St execs never hold themselves accountable. Not in 2008 and not now." Her words were retweeted over 2,500 times and more than 5,600 people "liked" them. Stumpf quit his 10-year tenure at the bank's helm less than a month later.

Apart from out-and-out greed, according to experts the growing divide between rich and poor is just one consequence of globalisation, there are many others. Parag Khanna has made a living out of analysing and predicting the dynamics and the likely outcomes our path is taking us down. I sat riveted as he presented his book *Connectography* at the 2016 Hay Festival. It draws upon a series of fascinating maps that illustrate how human life on earth is organized.[1] The emergence of new trade routes, logistics, supply chains and mass-migration; and the dominance of mega cities, digital connectivity, idea flows, automation, drones, driverless cars, demographics and changing values all feature. The book received mixed reviews but it nevertheless captures the fizzing cocktail of factors that are rapidly changing and disrupting our world.

It would be impossible to fully reflect all this change and its truly astonishing pace in this short book, but over the next few chapters I have attempted to describe some of the main drivers that are altering the world, and build a case for how something as simple as a Single Organizing Idea has the power to help business leaders concentrate their focus. I believe that the key drivers of change are:

- The reshaping of capitalism (discussed in Chapter 1)
- The waning of CSR (Chapter 2)
- The ascent of values (Chapter 3)
- The surge of technology (Chapter 4)
- The rise of reputation and fall of brand (Chapter 5).

---

* You can see the whole hearing on YouTube at: www.youtube.com/watch?v=xJhkX74D10M

Tellingly, Charles Darwin said, "It is not the strongest of the species that survive, nor the most intelligent, but the most responsive". As we go into this second part of the book have in mind which of the characters from our story is most likely to be responsive, and which of them is most characteristic of your business.

Is it Tomas Halle, the old-school CEO who's paying lip service to the new world order, but doesn't really get it and resents having to try? Or Conrad, the charismatic, influential and convention-breaking trailblazer, who's grasped the future early and is running with it, with all his considerable charm? Is it Mr Tang, the wise old owl who's so high up in the corporate stratosphere that he's seen the winds of change coming and is now trying to put radical reform in place in the only way he knows how: by firing and hiring? Or is it Bibi, our wide-eyed idealist Millennial; the plugged-in, tech-savvy social entrepreneur who "values values" and sees nothing but possibilities through the pursuit of a Single Organizing Idea?

1   The reshaping of capitalism

I want to tell you about a very large business that not only exists to make money, but also to make the world a better place. It's the second largest corporation in its sector in the world and it began trading in 1924.

From the beginning this company believed in employee wellbeing. So much so that it pioneered a shorter working week for its staff, along with higher wages, a full medical service and help with educational opportunities.

The company prospered over the next half century and in 1978 had to build a new factory to allow for expansion. On the same site, the company built gardens, kitchens and swimming pools for its employees, as well as football, hockey and cricket pitches; tennis and squash courts; a fishing lake and a bowling green. The company's ethos also led it to organize outings and even an annual summer camp for staff and their families.

The company was not happy with the standard of available social housing. So in 1993 it used profits to buy 120 acres of land and begin building homes. By 2000, 314 state-of-the-art houses with large gardens had been constructed on a 330-acre campus—not only for employees, but to create an environment in which a complete community could thrive. The company set up a trust to provide schools, hospitals, museums and a concert hall on the site. Today's campus contains 7,800 homes on 1,000 acres of land with 100 acres of parks and open space.

This is a business that could be said to exemplify "capitalism with a conscience". Can you name it? Maybe not, because I changed the dates to throw you off.

Cadbury* didn't begin trading in 1924, but 100 years earlier in 1824. It didn't build its new factory in 1978, but in 1878. And it was 1900 when its

---

* Cadbury's halo has slipped a bit recently. It was acquired by Kraft Foods in 2010 and demerged shortly after into Mondelez International (formerly Kraft Foods). According to Channel 4's current affairs programme 'Dispatches' Mondelez backtracked on the 'sincere belief' that the deal would save a Cadbury factory based in Somerdale near Bristol. 400 jobs were lost. For more details see www.telegraph.co.uk/food-and-drink/features/the-many-ways-cadbury-is-losing-its-magic/

workers started living in a model village called Bourneville on the outskirts of Birmingham, Britain's second largest city, not 2000.

So Cadbury's story doesn't portray our modern capitalist values, but rather the values and attitudes of some of our capitalist forefathers. The Quaker belief system that informed the purpose of successive generations of the Cadbury family also influenced the direction of several other household names including Barclays, Lloyds, Sony and John Hopkins and Cornell Universities. Cadbury's story gives us a glimpse of what capitalism meant to some and how it could be again, if only we wanted it that way. Interestingly, a growing groundswell of opinion does.

In January 2016 an Oxfam* report showed that the 62 richest billionaires on Earth own as much wealth as the poorer half of the entire world's population.[2] Moreover, the wealth of the poorest 50% dropped by two fifths between 2010 and 2015, despite an increase in the global population of 400 million. In the same period, the wealth of the richest 62 people increased by $500 billion to $1.76 trillion. For many, this is the face of capitalism today—and it's quite a contrast.

In the past, reports like these would have gone first to academics, journalists and sympathetic politicians but today, because the communications folk at Oxfam know what they're doing, this kind of information gets chopped up into sound-bites and jazzy infographics and sent straight to the general public.

The broad reaction is predictable—we all howl that the system is broken. It's left to the experts, those seeking a vote, or to sell their newspaper, to say, often in very roundabout ways, "Capitalism needs to be fixed." And I share the view that it can be, but only if it transforms into a more benign, agreeable version of itself.

In this chapter I'm sharing what some leading thinkers believe a better version of capitalism might look like.

The trouble with capitalism

First, let's check that we understand what is meant by "capitalism". The dictionary definition says that capitalism is "an economic and political system in which a country's trade and industry are controlled by private owners for profit, rather than by the state."

The bit I want to draw your attention to is "for profit". By definition, capitalists aims to make a profit, and that's all.

However, it's becoming clear that many of us are no longer happy when making a profit is the only thing that businesses do. We are also none too happy when businesses make too much profit, especially if it's at the expense

---

*   Oxfam also has Quaker roots as do the two other charity 'superbrands', Greenpeace and Amnesty.

of others. Remember in our story that FuelGlow is being held to account for making too much money at its customers' expense. In real life, these days, we regularly see examples of businesses being castigated for making so-called "excess profits" or taken to task for tax avoidance, which is entirely legal but no longer held to be *morally* acceptable. There has been a seismic shift in our attitudes towards businesses that look like they are only interested in making a profit.

By contrast, Conrad James' operation makes money too, but clearly the purpose of Soul House is quite different from FuelGlow's. He has aligned his enterprise with a new version of capitalism, which not only makes his endeavours palatable but popular, especially with our representative of the millennial generation, Bibi Okira.

One of the leading thinkers I alluded to earlier is Colin Mayer. Mayer is the Peter Moores Professor of Management Studies at the Saïd Business School in Oxford. In 2013 he published an enthralling book called *Firm Commitment.*[3] I gobbled it up in virtually one sitting and was quickly sold on what he had to say. Subsequently I went to hear him speak at the London School of Economics and, further inspired by his presentation, I introduced myself and asked for an interview. He obliged and a couple of weeks later I found myself sitting in his book-lined office.

Mayer's thesis is that while corporations have brought us many good things, including prosperity and employment, they're also responsible for much that's very bad, including poverty, pollution and a succession of financial crises. He believes that big business needs to change fundamentally and systemically if it's going to reverse the world-changing consequences of its activity.

His ambitious vision challenges government, business, consumers and shareholders to reconfigure companies and specifically the systems that govern their core purpose. A radical rethink, he says, is needed to bring down the existing apparatus and give birth to a new system that supports a new type of corporate enterprise: "a trust firm", which is interested in economies and society prospering equally.

According to Mayer, unless there's a fundamental root-and-branch change to the traditional way shares in companies are held, boards, directors and corporations simply can't change and will continue to fail us. He argues that dependence on "the market" won't get us where we need to be because "the market" only promotes good conduct in relation to the things that it itself values. It values profits, and therefore responds badly to anything that threatens the corporation's ability to earn profits.

Mayer asks us: "If the market values profit above all, do we share the same values?" The implied answer is "no, we don't". So Mayer is looking for corporations to revisit what they value and reform accordingly. As Su Lien Tang has recognized in our story, the pressure is on for businesses to change.

Shared value

On the other side of the Atlantic, further ideas are emerging on how to give birth to a new kind of capitalism. Professor Michael E Porter is ranked as one of the most influential thinkers of our time. In 2015, among many other accolades, he was voted the "Top Ranked Thinker of the Year" by Thinkers50,[4] a list described by *The Financial Times* as the "Oscars of management thinking". Together with Mark Kramer, the less well-known founder of the FSG consulting firm, the pair launched the Shared Value Initiative in 2011 through a *Harvard Business Review* article called: "Creating shared value: How to reinvent capitalism—and unleash a wave of innovation and growth".[5].

The article argued that capitalism is in need of reinvention because it's under siege as a result of people's diminished trust. Big business is widely believed to be the cause of social, environmental and economic problems (echoes of Mayer) and is also seen to be profiting at everyone else's expense (echoes of FuelGlow).

The lack of trust, moreover, is causing an entrenched adversarial relationship between governments and business. It leads governments to intervene to make corporates behave. Which is evidenced by the slew of regulations around, for instance, employee and environmental protection.

What's more, they say, the problem with capitalism is that it's compounded by business's narrow understanding of what matters: that its goal is simply to optimize short-term financial performance. This blinkered approach, according to Porter and Kramer, leads companies to overlook the wellbeing of their customers, the viability of their key suppliers, the sustainability of the natural resources they rely on and the economic vibrancy of the communities in which they operate.

This thinking is underpinned by a kind of universal assumption that it's not possible to pursue profit *and* do good in the world *at the same time.* What Porter and Kramer call "the presumed trade-off between economic efficiency and social progress."

The antidote to this assumption, they argue, is the pursuit of "Shared Value" which they define as: "creating economic value in a way that *also* creates value for society by addressing its needs and challenges." Shared Value, they add, isn't a form of social responsibility or philanthropy or sustainability (more on this in the next chapter). Rather it's something you put at the centre of what the business already does to achieve economic success.

Porter and Kramer claim that businesses have much to gain by addressing the world's problems. It gives them business opportunities and the chance to innovate and deliver solutions that both increase profits and contribute to society. It gives big business big issues to sink their teeth into—and they can use their innate abilities to make a substantial difference by delivering large-scale social and environmental benefits. The biggest draw of all is that Shared Value delivers the opportunity to gain competitive advantage.

Despite some criticisms (mainly from competing academics claiming plagiarism), I was compelled to learn more. So when I was invited to join a group of consultants from around the world and go to Boston in October 2015 and become a Shared Value Affiliate Consultant, I bought the air ticket and went for it.

The experience was valuable but I left with concerns. Despite Porter's assertion that "large companies are addressing big social problems as a core part of their strategy" in actual fact the Initiative's focus is on very clear specific measures that don't directly touch the core strategy of the business at all. The three recommendations are:

1   Reconceiving products and markets;
2   Redefining productivity in the value chain; and
3   Enabling local cluster developments to create "win-win" outcomes.

I argued this point of view directly with Kramer who had introduced himself by welcoming us to Harvard. I felt that unless the Shared Value ethos is embedded in the core of the business strategy, and until the entire business, from top to bottom, is organized and aligned with it, fundamental change can't and won't happen. By definition only the parts of the business that are directly affected by the three measures will change and behave differently, leaving the other parts, with no overall organizing idea to guide actions, to carrying on doing as they see fit. It could further exacerbate the negative silo thinking that many businesses struggle to deal with.

To be fair to Kramer he emphasized that the thinking behind the Initiative is very much a work in progress and it is interesting to remain a part of the Initiative if only to contribute ideas and see how it develops.

It would be nice to feel that small consultancies like my own and the other 23 affiliate consultancies selected to join the Shared Value network are helping shape Porter and Kramer's future thinking. But probably the greatest influence on them will come from the actions of the giant global corporates upon which their attention is primarily focused. In particular, actions like their potentially game-changing involvement in the shaping of the Sustainable Development Goals (SDGs).

Unlike the Millennium Development Goals that preceded them, big business was involved in the SDGs from their genesis and worked alongside governments and NGOs to determine their ambition. Interestingly Paul Polman, CEO of Unilever (who we will meet later in the chapter), and others don't think the SDGs go far enough. But the encouraging point is that they have been adopted and big businesses around the world are starting to think about how they align with them.

Corporates have understood for a long time that a degree of doing good is very much in their own best interests. What's exciting now is that the

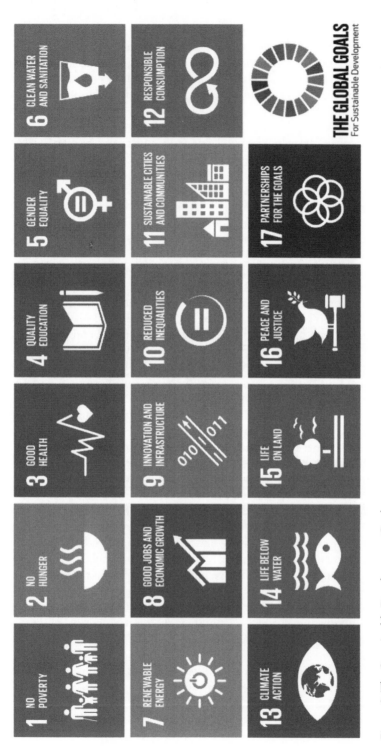

Figure 2 The Sustainable Development Goals

SDGs are helping them identify the big issues that will matter to their stakeholders going forward. In a sense the SDGs are acting as an organizing idea, perhaps even with the potential to give birth to something akin to the Quaker belief system: an ethos that will help create a shared purpose that all businesses—no matter their industry sector, size or location—can contribute to and align with.

Take for example Sustainable Development Goal number 13 (of 17): "Take urgent action to combat climate change and its impacts".[6] Climate change has a massive negative affect on the availability of key resources. The way it hurts the productivity of farmers is a case in point. Business is driven to act because making a change solves a problem for them as well as society. Originally launched in 2007, Marks & Spencer's Plan A 2020 is a prime example. Among the 100 revised and existing goals the British multinational high street retailer has set out to achieve is the systematic de-risking of its supply chain. It's a measure that includes actively encouraging and investing in helping their suppliers adapt to and mitigate climate change. This is exactly the "win-win" approach that both the authors of the SDGs and initiatives like Shared Value covet.

How on-board with the SDG agenda are big corporates? Well, we can get a sense of their attitude from a quote given by Barclays' Global Head of Citizenship and Reputation, Diane Eshelman, to the online sustainability platform 2degrees in July 2015. She said: "By making citizenship a part of everything we do, we build trust, differentiate ourselves from other banks, innovate our products and service, gain new customers and grow our business while also benefiting society."[7]

What's particularly exciting is that businesses can make such a profound difference. Companies like Marks & Spencer and Barclays who aim to operate this new version of capitalism will have the opportunity to deliver more impact than governments and NGOs combined. Ban Ki-moon, the UN Secretary-General, underlined this point in March 2015 when he said: "Business can make major contributions to widespread improvements in living standards. And markets are key to creating and diffusing solutions that will drive progress in our world. But this will not happen through 'business as usual'."[8] Indeed not.

Business has already made a massive contribution to the world. For example, corporations are largely responsible for building, developing and maintaining our modern-day transport, communications and energy infrastructures. As Parag Khanna pointed out, Vodafone built the mobile telecoms network in East Africa—not governments.[9] The number of corporations on our planet vastly dwarfs the number of non-profits, social-cause-driven enterprises, government schemes and foundations. Add in their supplier networks and their ability to influence customers and consumers, and corporations' reach far exceeds that of their public sector counterparts. Corporations reach down and put their products in the hands of billions of people, as well as their purpose in billions of hearts and minds. If they really want to change the world through a new version of capitalism I believe they can.

The trouble with change

All of which strikes a very optimistic note. However, even *Fortune* magazine's annual list of the 'Companies that Change the World' accepts that in reality almost all the featured businesses are compromised by legacy operations they've still not managed to change. By *Fortune's* own admission, its list includes companies that "compete in controversial industries or have engaged in harmful practices in some areas even as they create social benefits in others."[10]

What this tells us is that some of these businesses have still not changed at their core. Rather they've identified "win-wins" by adopting some of the three measures Porter and Kramer are advocating, thus being able to demonstrate innovation. This is not the same as total alignment with an SOI at the core of the business. Without a Single Organizing Idea holistically guiding the entire business the result is inevitably ad-hoc, predictably inconsistent, full of contradictions and unintended consequences.

"Win-win" when it suits them is undermining a potentially better version of capitalism and holding back the efforts of those choosing to lead. Society will not trust big business until big business demonstrates more convincingly that it is serious about its intention to make profit in order to make the world a better place. In the short-term, until the entire enterprise is engaged and driven by an SOI, businesses are open to accusations of cherry-picking the exercises and initiatives that suit them and ignoring others that don't.

It may be possible that over time the win-win profit and purpose outcomes of individual projects and activities will gradually change the mind-set and direction of an entire business. Over time, businesses may come to the conclusion that there is a business case for doing good and it can, "ultimately" (as the SDG Compass states), become part of their business strategy. But how long will that take and can the world wait?

Change we can believe in

The change that capitalist organizations are challenged with making is a radical one. But it's not impossible and Unilever—the world's third-largest consumer goods company—proves that it can be done, and at scale.

On 1 January 2009, Dutchman Paul Polman became CEO of Unilever. Almost immediately, he set a target to double the size of the company. At the same time he did something deeply unconventional. He argued that running a profitable business sustainably is vital for long-term growth. He pledged to reduce Unilever's environmental footprint while improving its social impact through the company's core strategy: the 'Sustainable Living Plan'. "The more our products meet social needs and help people live sustainably," he explained, "the more popular our brands become and the more we will grow".

Of course sceptical shareholders were alarmed that his profit and purpose approach would lead to disaster. They believed the financial performance of Unilever was at risk, and were increasingly rattled when he scrapped all CSR and philanthropic ventures, as well as short-term financial reporting.

Yet his strategy has paid dividends in every way. It didn't happen overnight, but Polman understood the long-term benefit. "Who says a purpose-driven business can't be profitable?" he asked in 2015,[11] five years after first implementing the strategy and once it was beginning to show results. Polman's unprecedented determination and leadership had led him to a huge battle with his own board, had him to face up to his investors and call out their focus on short-term financial performance. Ultimately he demonstrated that an alternative way is sustainable. Not just in monetary terms but, equally importantly, on a societal level too.

Investors will always be concerned about whether a new approach to business can translate into growth. By year six, however, Unilever's results were described by its investors as "reasonable". So is Unilever in fact behaving like the "trust firm" that Professor Colin Mayer talks about? Well, Paul Polman is doing a good job. It's by no means an amazing success story, and it's vital that we're realistic here. Profit and purpose is not a magic bullet that will turn social purpose into instant short-term wealth. But perhaps neither should we be looking for that anymore.

Unilever is not perfect and it may even be that there's no such thing as a whiter than white company. However in a recent series of interviews that I conducted with a number of America's biggest global corporations, one senior executive described Unilever as "the trailblazers". Unilever is proactive business on the leading edge, not a reactive follower waiting to see how things pan out. Throughout the course of my interviews, many contributors cited Unilever and named Paul Polman as the poster child of a new version of capitalism. This will satisfy a man who has declared that he will have failed if he only changes his own company. His ambition is systemic change for the whole fast-moving consumer goods (FMCG) sector and its entire supply chain.

What's more, these new ideas are spreading. "A noteworthy trend has emerged over the past 10 years, and it is on a steady and rapid incline," *Fast Company* magazine pointed out in May 2015.[12] "Companies," it continued, "have started to realize that profit and purpose (aka social impact) can and should go hand in hand. Rather than separating the revenue-generating side of the business from the philanthropic side, socially progressive companies are thinking of them as co-existent, and in the process, generating greater impact and revenue than they would by keeping them separate."

This kind of thinking is building in momentum and is on the cusp of seeping into the mainstream. Mayer's "trust firms" and Porter and Kramer's Shared Value Initiative are part of a wider groundswell of recent activity that includes other prominent contributions from fledgling organizations such as B Team, B Lab, the Conscious Business movement, Social Innovation, Social Entrepreneurship, Social Enterprise, Inclusive Business, Triple Bottom Line and Net Positive. These organizations are collectively reshaping capitalism into something the Cadbury founders would recognize and the majority of people seem to want.

The financial 2008 crisis hasn't thrown up an alternative to capitalism. Instead the crisis, and the other drivers of change I will look at in the following chapters, is resulting in the promise of a better version of capitalism. One that will hopefully be with us fairly soon.

An SOI is a management tool that has the potential to make sense of a host of profit/social purpose initiatives and help achieve their shared ambition to change the world for good.

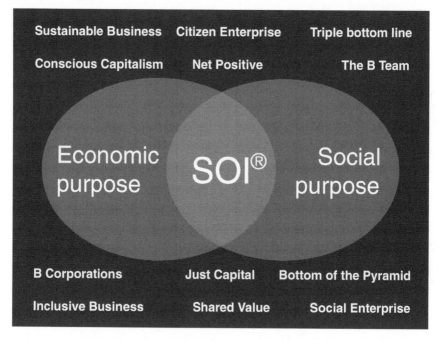

Figure 3 The potential of a Single Organizing Idea

2   The waning of CSR

The revenge of the pukeko

A decade ago an extremely resourceful pukeko minced across the television screens of New Zealanders and into their hearts. The clever creatives at Lowe Advertising had co-opted the cute NZ bird and convinced it to be filmed out and about collecting an array of eclectic materials for its nest. Their client was Genesis Energy and the message was that they generated power from more sources than anyone else in an attempt to establish themselves as a responsible green energy company.

Remarkably, within weeks the very same bird got another gig doing exactly the same thing. But this time for an entirely different organization. In Greenpeace's spoof take-off of the original ad the bird explains that it had in fact been ordered to pick up pegs and steal laces from people's shoes; and that further, this was all part of a cynical attempt by Genesis Energy to infer that its power came from multiple sources when in fact 75% of it came from climate killing coal and gas. "At Genesis we put profits ahead of sustainability" stated the revised sign off.

Of course the video went viral and Genesis found itself joining a long list of big-name organizations that have had their wings clipped by exaggerating corporate social responsibility (CSR) claims.

The list includes British Airways (BA). In 2005 the airline made a bold commitment to offset all of its carbon emissions. Did the airline do this with the best will in the world? I honestly don't know. But we do know that the programme foundered badly, because it came to light in 2007 that BA had only offset 3,000 tonnes of emissions, an embarrassing 0.01% of the total emissions burden,[1] equivalent to a mere one day's worth of flights between London and New York. So BA got lambasted for lying, because they did. And because that's how CSR can go.

Next comes Walmart. A highly publicised commitment to energy-saving light bulbs appeared to be a "win-win" CSR strategy for the retail giant. Unfortunately, Walmart's efforts were completely undermined when its US staff went on strike demanding a fair wage. This coincided with allegations of corruption within the company's Mexico operations. Far from making negative publicity go away, CSR efforts on one front had rather tended to draw attention to the organization's less stellar performance in another area of its operations.

Corporate history is littered with similar examples. Automobile manufacturer Volkswagen (VW) spectacularly fell from grace as a consequence of engineering a green image built on a deliberate and frankly staggering lie. In September 2015 the US Environmental Protection Agency (EPA) announced that it had found software code built into VW's diesel cars that cheated emissions testing. The scandal immediately cost the CEO his job and some estimates predict it will cost the company up to $18 billion.

In this chapter I am not arguing that organizations should walk away from CSR, but that it must take a much clearer-eyed view of the role it plays in their business. In other words, is CSR part and parcel of the core purpose of your business and something that you single-mindedly organize around, or is it a disconnected activity that is bolted onto your business in an attempt to enhance reputation in pursuit of profit?

If it is a bolt-on, in our connected world, expect to be called out. A veritable online cottage industry of activists and "greenwash debunkers" exists to unmask you. "You just can't argue against a company that spends a bit of cash on the community", says Tomas Halle, the CEO stereotype in our story. How wrong he is.

What exactly is CSR?

Let's start by noting that just as the next iteration of capitalism has an array of monikers, so too does CSR. Labels include "corporate conscience", "corporate citizenship", "social performance", "responsible business" and "corporate social innovation". You could argue that the mutability of the name says something about the mutability of what people mean by it. You could also argue that for want of a universally agreed name, the practice of CSR has been inconsistent and variable and that has counted against it. But that's an argument for later in this chapter.

For now, if we broadly understand "corporate social responsibility" as a range of "responsible" activities—what then does that cover? Like the name it's a bit fluid. For instance, some count philanthropy and volunteering, as CSR and some don't. I personally understand CSR most clearly when I think of it as any activity which makes an organization more sustainable. While sustainability has been discussed for many years, as a concept that nations discuss together, it has its roots in the 1972 Stockholm Conference on the Human Environment. That was the very first time an international gathering discussed how human activity was negatively impacting the planet. However, for a more official definition I've gone to ISO 26000, the international standard that exists to provide organizations of all sizes and types with "guidelines for social responsibility". According to the standard—which is written by global experts—"The objective of social responsibility is to contribute to sustainable development."[2]

The standard goes on to list "the core subjects pertaining to social responsibility", which I'm quoting here at length, because I think the breadth of issues covered is interesting and possibly goes beyond the popular perception of CSR. They are:

- **Human rights,** including civil, political, economic, social and cultural rights, and rights at work
- **Labour practices,** including health and safety at work, employment relationships, employment conditions and training in the workplace
- **The environment,** including pollution prevention, sustainable resource use, climate change mitigation and adaptation, protection of biodiversity and restoration of natural habitats
- **Fair operating practices,** including anti-corruption, fair competition and promoting social responsibility in the value chain
- **Consumer issues,** including fair marketing and contractual practices, protecting consumers' health and safety, consumer data protection and privacy and providing access to essential services
- **Community involvement and development,** including education and culture, employment creation and skills development, technology development and access, health, and wealth and income creation.

Finally, and here's the rub, CSR is also whatever a business wants it to be. It's self-regulated, so enterprises can choose whichever interpretation of CSR they care to adopt (ISO 26000 is entirely voluntary); and they can implement CSR however they wish. As I've suggested, such infinite flexibility is probably both a strength and a weakness. It leads to widely variable approaches, impacts and benefits of CSR, as Dr Mark Wade, a colleague and friend, explains in the next section.

How CSR is done

Mark Wade is a renowned expert in sustainability. His experience started in the late 1990s with Royal Dutch Shell as Head of Sustainable Development Strategy, Policy & Reporting and subsequently Head of Sustainable Development Learning. In this role the thinking that he developed won Shell wide recognition as a sustainability trailblazer at a time when corporations had little understanding of the subject. At its most basic, Wade explains, "we very quickly saw that to be authentic sustainability thinking had to be fully integrated into business strategy, daily operations, leadership and culture. Anything else was missing the point. We were at odds with the then trendy CSR movement with its misconstrued notion of doing social good almost as a pay-back to society—a form of corporate philanthropy and/or social investment."[3] This he believes is peripheral to the purpose and daily operations of the organization and will deliver only limited beneficial impacts.

Shell saw that society was—and is increasingly—expecting more of companies; to be responsible for all activities and impact—economic, environmental and social—and to be part of the solution to world needs, not the problem.

Shell's Social Performance Management Unit took a hard look at the range of ways in which companies devote time and money to society. They saw a continuum that they dubbed "the social investment wedge"—see Figure 4.

At its most basic is "corporate philanthropy"—find a good cause, any good cause, write the cheque and walk away. There is minimal engagement around social or community needs and often no relationship to the activities or impacts of the company.

Then there is "social investment", where companies identify a good cause and support it in partnership with societal organisations. There is some engagement and money is usefully targeted but it is of limited value to society and the company, except for a bit of good PR. The activity is usually administered by a special department distant from daily operations.

Next comes what Shell dubbed "strategic social investment". Here there is a deliberate effort to understand the needs of local/regional communities impacted by a site of operation and to provide practical support to meets those needs. The effort is integrated into local management decisions and requires a high level of engagement with local stakeholders. The value to both company and community is high as local needs and concerns are addressed (typically employment, training, local procurement, reduced environmental impacts and social development) and the company earns a critical "license to operate" with reduced risk and cost.

Finally, there "social impact management", where the company takes a holistic view of the needs of a country in which it is operating (or ultimately to its place in the world if a global player) and relates this to its competences and impacts.[4,5] The conversation is strategic and aligned to core purpose. Insights are used to configure how business strategy, capabilities and impacts can be aligned with societal needs. The value to the society is matched by the value to the company where its presence, products and services are valued and the company becomes first choice for consumers, employees, investors and partners. This is a world away from traditional CSR and moves the conversation on from doing good to the alignment of company strategy and purpose with an SOI that provides sustainable solutions to societal needs.

Shell's Social Impact Management is aligned to core purpose. It is a "world away from traditional CSR and moves the conversion on from 'doing good' to the alignment of company strategy and purpose to social needs".

Social Investment Wedge

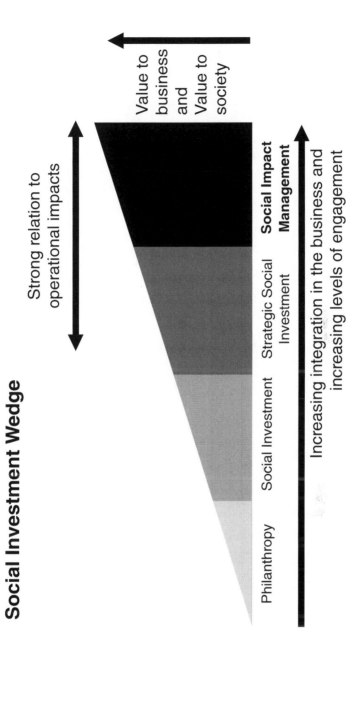

Figure 4 Shell's social investment wedge

The trouble with CSR

Paul Polman, who we briefly met in Chapter 1, agrees. The problem with traditional CSR, whatever the level, is that the effort is occasional and *ad hoc*, carried out when and where it suits the company. In May 2016 he said as much in an interview with the *Huffington Post*. "Most companies understand that they have to be part of the solution," he explained, "but often the focus is still on occasional CSR, rather than fully embedding sustainability into the business model and working with others to drive transformational change."[6]

A key objection to CSR, then, is that it's an optional bolt-on, as I mentioned earlier. It's not core to the business. For Polman, the whole business has to be driven by a core idea such as his own Sustainable Living Plan (USLP). USLP is, in effect, Unilever's SOI and, in Unilever's case, there is clear evidence that the pursuit of it is delivering the goods. Asked in the same interview about the most important thing he's done at Unilever, Polman answered, "…most importantly helped develop a new business model that serves society first and foremost." He added: "Increasingly we are showing that a more purpose-driven model makes a lot of business sense." In other words a model that has an SOI at its core is driving both profit and purpose equally.

While some are sceptical of initiatives like Shared Value—"I see it as a sophisticated form of greenwashing" said one senior executive of a Fortune 500 company I interviewed in 2016—no such accusation is levelled at Polman's approach. "We are inspired by what is happening at Unilever and moving away from traditional CSR thinking" the executive explained. "Everything we now start is led by the human point of view first and that is totally revolutionising what we do and how we do it. Embedding this thinking into the core of our business is not yet there but it's on the agenda—it's what we want to achieve."

Getting a move on

A second big problem with CSR is that it's too little, too slowly. As another Fortune 500 senior executive I interviewed noted: "'Doing good' is out of date. What we actually need to do is fix things because if we don't we—as human beings—are going to be in a great deal of trouble."

Joel Makower, GreenBiz's Group Executive Editor, underlined the point in 2014. "While more and more companies are undertaking a growing number of initiatives to reduce their environmental impacts," he said, "there's very little progress to show for it. Company initiatives are not having an impact at the scale needed to address such challenges as climate change and the availability of water and natural resources."[7]

And those challenges are mounting. According to GreenBiz, greenhouse gasses have grown nearly twice as fast over the past decade as they did in the preceding 30 years. This despite the global financial crisis and resulting economic slowdown. We are also extracting 50% more natural resources each year than we were 30 years ago.

Another warning comes from Peter Bakker, President of the World Business Council for Sustainable Development. Ahead of COP 21, the 2015 UN Climate Change Conference held in Paris, he said: "To avert the most serious consequences of climate change, we must stay under the 2°C limit for global warming. A massive transformation of our economies, policies and societies is necessary to make this happen." Commenting on day one of the conference Sir David Attenborough, the world- renowned broadcaster and naturalist chillingly summed it up in an interview with BBC Breakfast: "We've got a decade."

A few months later, in November 2015, Barclays Bank put on the hubristically titled: 'Greatest debate in sustainability history', which pitted leading sustainability thinker John Elkington against Shared Value's Mark Kramer to debate 'Is CSR dead?'

"We are in the emergency ward on planet earth," said Elkington. "There are three large constituents that can address the issue: one is government, one is civil society and one is business. But unless we see systemic change to the way every business contributes we are lost."[8]

Back in 1988 Elkington had published a book called *The Green Consumer Guide: How to buy goods that don't cost the Earth*.[9] Critiquing the book, journalist Richard Gosden noted: "The idea is that when awareness of environmental problems penetrates deeply enough into the community consciousness the purchasing power of the mass market will force all manufacturers to green both their products and the manufacturing processes on pain of being rejected."[10]

This green consumer movement emerged in about 1987, the year Anita Roddick's The Body Shop won 'Company of the Year' in the UK Business Enterprise Awards. The movement grew and by 1989 Gosden had it that the mainstream media were "falling over themselves" in a rush to inform citizens of their responsibility to consume responsibly. Lists appeared around the world. The UK's Total Environment Centre published "The shopping list that saves the world". On the other side of the planet we got "Shopping with a Conscience: A guide to who's who behind the products Australians buy". But then things started to go awry.

By 1991 the movement had run its course, brought down by a sceptical media, which wrote influential articles highlighting the unintended and harmful side effects of some green products. Planet-damaging manufacturing processes and the lack of supply-chain transparency were also highlighted. A final nail in the coffin were the misleading claims made by "high-priests of over consumption", that is to say, the advertising industry, which played the "green image game".

Which brings us back full circle to our pukeko.

A short time after the pukeko had had its revenge an email pinged into my inbox. Despite the curious name of the sender this was not a spoof: Pattrick Smellie was the Brand and Communications Director of New Zealand's second largest listed company, and its biggest energy sector generator and retailer—Contact Energy. The lunch he invited me to would lead me to the centre of the CSR debate at the heart of the country I'd been living in for three years. A country that, at the time, really hadn't fully explained what it meant by describing itself as "100% Pure".[11]

As a brand strategist my task was to help Contact position itself favourably in the minds of its stakeholders. As part of the task and in an effort to make solid recommendations to Contact's executive team, Pattrick and I pored over CSR research gathered from experts and academics from around the world. We also conducted our own research.

What we found was this: despite the best efforts of Genesis and others in NZ's highly competitive energy sector, no advantage was to be gained by claiming to be greener than the competition. One source stated that "...the success of a brand strategy which positions the product exclusively on its functional attributes may be limited by the fact that the reduction of a product's environmental impact generally does not deliver individual benefits to the buyer. Therefore, the perceived customer benefit may be insufficient as a motivating factor to purchase...".[12] At the end of the day what consumers actually wanted was cheap energy, reliably delivered.

So despite the huge temptation to influence consumer preference and government policy (the NZ government was writing its Sustainable Energy Strategy that year) by pursuing a "me too" course that followed their competitors, through my hypothesis presentation I convinced the CEO and his team that they should harness energy in a different way. "Positivity" was born as the firm's SOI.

The bottom line was that while Contact could implement CSR initiatives that would put its competitors in the shade, it wasn't the right thing to do. Research had shown that while both corporate executives and consumers believed that obligations to shareholders must be balanced with contributions to the broader good, any attempt to leverage that with bolt-on CSR would be met with derision. In a nutshell what was required was simply that the business behaved ethically in everything it did from its core outward.

Pattrick and I were certainly not alone in advocating a more systemic approach to sustainable business that worked for all stakeholders. On the other side of the world in Bristol, UK, Nick Davies was making similar recommendations. Only Nick was coming at it from the ground up.

Nick was running a communications agency specialising in an approach he called "localisation". He recognised that as the world became more global, companies were losing touch with "local". All around the world people were feeling increasingly forgotten as big business moved out of town, causing high streets to decline, facilities to close and transport links to be withdrawn. This betrayal of community was eroding trust to such an extent that citizens were starting to question whether these global brands had any relevance in their lives any more.

Some companies had spotted this trend and were launching community engagement programmes but these were prohibitively expensive to do at scale—it was simply impossible to find, manage and report on hundreds of community projects using manual processes alone. Disturbingly for Nick, some were now trying to get around this problem by launching community competitions in an effort to land a national message of local support.

As Nick explains, "A community competition initially seems like a good idea for a company. They can create a powerful image of care and concern via a dedicated microsite, use their marketing channels to promote it and capture entries (and data of course) as they roll in. It can generate valuable content too because every community in the land needs a little money to patch up the community centre, run a community bus and so on, and communities will work hard on their entries to demonstrate the extent of local support. After all, every local community needs all the help it can get."

And this is where things start to unravel. "No matter the size of your fund, a competition creates significantly more losers than winners" says Nick. "The disappointment of missing out on the free holiday offered by your daily breakfast cereal rarely rocks anybody's world. But if you're a neighbourhood group galvanised in a battle to keep the community shop open because the local council has just withdrawn funding—well, that's very different". Add the fact that competition microsites typically announce "this competition is currently closed" for the majority of the year and an already contentious CSR initiative rapidly becomes capable of doing more brand harm than good.

So how do you make it safe for any company to travel the long road to transformation when surrounded by such doubtful stakeholders? Like many purposeful business advocates before him, Nick's concern was that such experiences would make the journey feel too hard. His solution was simple—strength in numbers. Nick launched Neighbourly.com in 2014 as a place for businesses to sit side-by-side and collaborate with society on ever-more ambitious community initiatives that would eventually consign CSR to history. Much has been achieved already and we'll re-visit Neighbourly towards the end of this book to learn more.

To be sustainable, organizations don't need CSR. They need to be somewhat approved of and accepted in the communities where they operate and to be careful stewards of their environment and of finite resources. This is not achieved by CSR. It comes from being ethical, which comes from values, the subject of our next chapter.

3   The ascent of values

Saints and sinners

Long ago a man named Gerald Ratner stepped on to a podium and in a truly remarkable fashion claimed the title of "Biggest blunderer in corporate history." He still holds that title today, though there have been several challengers.

When Ratner took up his position on the podium at the Royal Albert Hall on the 29 April 1991 he was at the peak of his career. He had taken his sleepy family jewellery business and made it into a world-beater. With 1,000 shops in the UK and a similar number in the USA, Ratner was one of the few businessmen to have made it on both sides of the Atlantic. The Ratner Group was the biggest jewellery business in the world and its CEO one of the most celebrated.

But in the space of 25 minutes everything he had built was destroyed.

In the audience that evening were 5,000 members of the UK's prestigious Institute of Directors, a member of the Royal Family and a handful of journalists. They were eager to learn about the secret behind Ratner's success and he was happy to tell them. "We sell total crap," he said. "Honestly, we do." Encouraged by the gales of laughter his candour received he pressed on, listing item after item from his "crap stock list". The inference was clear—his customers were idiots and they were being duped.

In bragging about how he had created value for his shareholders he had displayed his own values. The impact was immediate and seismic. The day after the night before £500m (£750m today) was wiped off the value of the business. Within a year most of his shops had closed down with the loss of hundreds of jobs. Ratner was forced to resign and the company changed its name.

Ryanair CEO Michael O'Leary challenged hard for Ratner's title for many years until he had a change of heart and direction. Where Ratner preyed on his customers' ignorance, O'Leary preyed on his customers' vulnerability. Hidden charges, customer fines, discrimination, abusive customer service, breaking aviation safety rules, poor treatment of staff and several court cases were the hallmarks of a business that wallowed in controversy and contempt for its customers. *The Economist* described the Irish carrier as "having a deserved reputation for nastiness"[1] and Which?, Britain's leading consumer association, ranked it "the worst firm for customer service".[2]

But O'Leary didn't make gaffes and he didn't make blunders. His outlandish behaviour was deliberate and the outcomes calculated. He felt safe calling his passengers "idiots" and telling the media that they were "stupid" for being fined for not bringing their boarding passes to the airport. Free PR and newspaper inches seemed a reasonable payoff—that was until the oil price changed and the profit warnings arrived. When that happened Ryanair took swift measures to improve its image and tackle the impact that years of profit before people had had on its reputation. In 2014 at the airline's AGM, in the face of falling profits, O'Leary threw in the towel and declared that his business would no longer "unnecessarily piss people off". Europe's biggest carrier, he said, would become "family friendly". It softened its position on baggage charges and booking conditions, overhauled its website and introduced allocated seating, a new business class service and a family discount scheme.

"As I said myself if I had known being nicer to our customers was going to work so well I would have done it years ago," said O'Leary without a trace of irony.[3] His forced about-turn on his values brought Ryanair back from the brink. From now on, it would take a page out of a different budget airline's book, that of America's Southwest Airlines whose values put people first, "connecting people to what's important in their lives through friendly, reliable and low-cost air travel."[4]

Tony Hayward, meanwhile, did make a gaffe. In fact, the then CEO of BP made a series of gaffes following the 2010 Deepwater Horizon explosion which caused the biggest oil spill in marine drilling history. Eleven people were killed and the environment and livelihoods of thousands of people were devastated. Yet among Hayward's responses was a remark on live television that what he wanted was "*his* life back".

The blunder led a predatory American media to dig up his past and it didn't take long for them to find damning evidence with which to further tarnish the Brit. In a lecture given to Stanford Business School students in 2009, Hayward boasted that until he took over, BP had been heading in the wrong direction. "Too many people were working to save the world," he said, adding: "We'd lost track of the fact that our primary purpose in life is to create value for our shareholders." His values, which put profit first, ultimately cost Hayward his job.

The purpose of values

In his 2012 book, *What Matters Now,* pioneering American management consultant Gary Hamel writes: "If you are the leader at any level in an organization, you are a steward of careers, capabilities, resources, the environment and organizational values.".[5] I would be explicit and add that you are also the steward of the purpose of the organization. He goes on, "Unfortunately not every manager is a wise steward. Some behave like mercenaries—by mortgaging the future to inflate short-term earnings, by putting career ahead of the company, by exploiting vulnerable employees, by preying on customer ignorance, or by manipulating the political system in ways that reduce competition."

What's interesting is that all three of our "sinners" ran businesses that had very clear and honourable purposes. Ratner's was to make jewellery affordable for all. O'Leary to deliver cheap travel for all and Hayward to go "Beyond Petroleum". Ratner and O'Leary pursued their purposes with total disregard for stewardship of principles and Hayward disregarded stewardship of both purpose and principles.

Lord Browne, Hayward's predecessor and the architect of "Beyond Petroleum" had stated on the company's website that: "Our core values are at the heart of everything we do, guiding our decision making and giving our business a clear sense of direction". But stewardship of these organizational values had not been undertaken and they were quickly lost, as Hayward's Stanford speech revealed. In 2005 BP was involved in another explosion, this time at the Texas City Refinery. It killed five people. A year later in an interview with *Fortune* magazine a BP employee who wished to remain anonymous revealed an interesting insight into what really drove the business: "Constant turnover only worsened matters, as new bosses would seek to beat the previous manager's numbers. The values are real, but they haven't been aligned with our business practices in the field."[6]

Barclays Bank also had values that got lost in time. CEO Anthony Jenkins made it his mission to restore them. It was a cause that earned him the nickname "Saint Anthony". The Barclays name had been tarnished for some time. Since it was tagged "Boerclays" in the 1980s because of its association with South Africa's apartheid government, Barclays had courted controversy. Accusations of money laundering, excessive bonus payments, tax avoidance, poor customer service, conflicts of interest, market manipulation and fraud were all thrown at the bank.

In a 244-page report into Barclays' business practices ordered by the City of London, lawyer Anthony Salz concluded that "Significant failings developed in the organization as it grew. The absence of a common purpose or common set of values has led to conduct problems, reputational damage and a loss of public trust".[7]

Much of the blame was put on the poisonous culture created during the reign of Bob Diamond, Jenkins' high profile American predecessor. Under his tenure, in a quest for growth seemingly at all costs, the bank welded together two very different types of banking and two diametrically opposed cultures—investment and retail banking.

Like our other sinners Diamond received widespread criticism in the media for his perceived lack of humility, his huge pay packet and his arrogance (according to the BBC, in 2011 Diamond earned £20.9m[8]). Lord Peter Mandelson, the UK's Business Secretary at the time described Diamond as "the unacceptable face of banking." Like Wells Fargo's John Stumpf, Diamond resigned following a government select committee hearing not unlike the one our CEO Tomas Halle sat through in our story.

Taking over, Jenkins set out his vision for a new kind of banking—one based on the values of the bank's Quaker founders. In a speech on "Driving competitive advantage through values-based leadership", made shortly after his appointment to the Carnegie Council for Ethics in International Affairs, Jenkins told those gathered, "The one thing that we all know is that you can't guarantee that things will remain the same in life. Life changes and you have to change with it, but always with the values as the guiding star. The way you respond to that change has to be in line with the core values of the organization." He went on, "There is a saying that great companies change everything except their values. If you have a value system that can stand the test of time, through thick and thin, that keeps people grounded and focused on what they are doing, then I believe you will succeed."

Values as lodestar

Jenkins' tenure at Barclays didn't last long. His lack of strategic drive to grow Barclays' investment banking activities—the business Diamond had built—was the main reason given for his sacking. He moved onto a new post, chairing the Prince of Wales' Business in the Community initiative. Their Chief Executive, Stephen Howard, said of his appointment: "The ability of business leaders to ensure that their values influence the behaviour of their business means that they are at the heart of rebuilding trust in business and making responsible leadership the norm."[9] Unfortunately Jes Staley, the man who took over from the ousted Jenkins looks like he may not have that ability. Less than 18 months into the job he is being investigated by financial regulators after admitting trying to unmask a whistleblower.[10]

FuelGlow's old-school CEO Tomas Halle would probably meet Howard's words with rolling eyes and abject cynicism. What he values above all else is the creation of wealth and, most importantly, his personal ability to create it. Like Ratner and O'Leary, he boasts of his success—for him the creation of profit is what makes him a great leader—a point he makes to his employer.

But times are quickly changing and values are becoming increasingly important and potent. Values are increasingly used to assess the behavior of companies and how we judge them. For example, Britain's biggest supermarket, Tesco, was in the doghouse in 2015 when it was revealed that it had systematically withheld payments from its suppliers to improve its financial position. In one case Tesco withheld a multimillion-pound payment to one supplier for more than two years. Once made public through a highly critical report,[11] Tesco had nowhere to hide. Understanding that any kind of further denial was futile it set up an online Supplier Network to recast its relationships with its suppliers and in repeated statements through various media it was forced to accept that its behavior reflected values that were widely viewed to be unacceptable.

Values are important because they provide a kind of lodestar that everyone in the business can follow. Values keep people on track and they help ensure the consistent delivery of positive experiences. But only if you adhere to them.

In 2002 Arthur Andersen, one of the biggest of the "big five" accountancy firms, voluntarily relinquished its license and ceased to exist anywhere but on paper. A year earlier I had been preparing to take over leadership of the project team at the WPP-owned global brand consultancy* responsible for creating Andersen's brand strategy.

It was an exciting time as the work was poised to radically change the face of the entire sector across the globe. But it never happened. As I discussed Andersen's new look and the strategy behind it with Andersen's communications team in our London board room, three thousand miles away in Chicago panic had broken out. The ink had barely dried on the value statements penned by our brand strategists when the fateful news came that the firm was in desperate trouble. Enough trouble for the communications team to immediately head back home. It later transpired that two of Andersen's executives had ordered the shredding of thousands of documents in an effort to cover up financial reporting irregularities related to their client, Enron. As a colleague jokingly pointed out to me, the irony was that their actions had aligned almost perfectly with one of the five values about to be adopted by the firm: "No. 5: MAVERICK. We have always taken what we believe to be the right course of action, even when it was contrary to established ways. Driven by integrity, we continue to challenge the system and open new pathways."

Clairvoyant powers were at work—they couldn't have seen the new values—but clearly they had missed the all-important third word of the second sentence.

The point is that even if they had read the values statements, would it have made a difference? Peter Drucker, the recognized founder of modern management theory, famously said "Culture eats strategy for breakfast".[12]

I learned a lot during my time with WPP in the early 2000s—I learned what worked and what didn't work. Primarily what I learned was the importance of the pursuit of the truth. Values cannot be manufactured like flags of convenience cynically flown to give off the "right impression". They need to be rooted in reality and reflect the true nature of the business.

Businesses that need to change to remain relevant of course need to adapt but the core values of a business should never change. They should remain

---

*   Enterprise IG, later renamed Brand Union.

a permanent guide, part of the core idea around which everything the business does is focused.

The fact that so many of the world's leading businesses are now changing is an indication of just how many have lost their original values or frankly didn't have them in the first place. This creates a huge problem of credibility and it can be no surprise that digitally connected employees inside, and consumers with axes to grind on the outside, are quick to call out anything they see as "fluff" or cynical attempts at reinvention.

Change has to take place and both IBM and Unilever have proved that it can be done (see Chapter 4 for more details about IBM's work to redefine its purpose). In reframing the vision of the future around which they are organized, both corporations reassessed the values and behaviors that could help them achieve it. I personally believe that Lord Browne and his call to go "Beyond Petroleum" was ahead of his time. IBM and Unilever have the benefit of a much greater understanding and insight into where the world is really heading (Browne was still dealing in theory), and the shifting attitudes and behaviours that our global community expects.

Shifting sands

We can get a good insight into these new attitudes from the JUST Capital Foundation's research.* Set up in April 2014 by billionaire hedge fund manager, Paul Tudor Jones, and philosophical idealist, Deepak Chopra, JUST Capital aims to create a new kind of stock market index that drives capital to companies recognized for treating their employees and communities well.

Their extensive research studies** clearly indicate that corporations whose values emphasize employee satisfaction, together with betterment of society as a whole, are benefiting from both tangible and intangible results. The headline findings are interesting, and underline the fact that we live in a climate that is increasingly demanding change:

- The public does not think that corporations are currently prioritizing the right stakeholders. Regardless of political ideology, respondents feel that corporations should ideally prioritize customers, communities, employees and the environment more than they do now
- Large majorities of every traditional ideological grouping agree with the statement that "a company should get credit for improving the way it affects people or the environment, even if it still has some problems"
- A strong majority of respondents in every income group say measuring "just" corporate behaviour is important

---

* For more information, see: https://justcapital.com/
** Completed in September 2015, involving 43,000 respondents representative of US census demographic and ideological markers.

- A clear majority of people in every traditional ideological grouping say that if they had information on how "just" a corporation is, it would have at least some influence on their decisions to work for, buy from, or invest in that corporation.

For Jones, the message is clear. "Companies that treat their employees and society well will see better financial results over the long term."[13] As JUST Capital's corporate video explains, by giving power to people to make decisions based on their values, in turn consumers, workers, investors, corporate leaders and concerned citizens will change businesses and "create an economy that works for all of us." At his TED talk in March 2015, Tudor Jones went on to say: "When we put justice on a par with profit, we will get back our humanity."

Millennial values

In fact, Jones' findings confirm quite a striking shift in values. Moreover, this striking shift is likely to be amplified by a specific group of people, represented in our story by the Millennial—Bibi Okira.

When Browne was re-launching BP in 2000 the last of the Millennial's were just being born. Millennials—people born between 1980 and 2000—are particularly influential because according to a PwC report quoted in B Team's *New Ways of Working* report, in a number of countries they're expected to make up 50% of the workforce by 2020, and 75% of the global workforce by 2025.[14] Clearly their values matter. So here's an important one: 92% of Millennials reject the idea that profit should be the sole measure of success for a business.[15] According to Nielsen, Millennials are also four times more responsive than older people to a company with sustainability credentials.[16]

Bibi represents the values of her generation. Everything she hears at the FutureWorks Hybrid Seminar resonates with her. She regards the case for profit and purpose, as laid out by Conrad James and embodied in the success of his company, as a road map for her own ambitions.

It isn't a question of converting Bibi to a cause, and the same applies to many of her generation. This is about crystalizing a growing human desire to do business in a new way. Conrad James simply puts it into words, and lets both reputation and long-term results do the real talking.

Meanwhile Bibi is easily carried along: Millennials make decisions using both their hearts and minds. Millennials are also highly digitally active. They communicate and connect fast and make Snapchat-speed decisions. Instead of reading, their media of choice satisfies their needs through sound bites and "see bites". So we can surmise that Millennials generally come to conclusions based on limited information and rely more on the feelings generated by what they see and hear. This is evidenced by the 17th Edelman Trust Barometer,[17] presented by its founder Richard Edelman during the

2017 World Economic Forum held in Davos. This showed that Millennials are more trusting of digital media than the general public as a whole.* This matters because this new generation is one that the older generation of CEOs is trying to engage.

In our story, it's safe to say that Conrad James is engaging successfully with Bibi. His organization is smart, progressive and connected, just like Bibi herself. But as well, its aspirations and values—to be fiscally successful and a force for good in society—resonate with her. It's quite evident from Bibi's response that she admires the work of the figure behind an organization that makes money and a difference. That Conrad James is talking about long-term growth over short-term profits doesn't faze her. Bibi recognizes that this is the only sustainable option. She shares Conrad James' values on having a long-term positive impact.

The real thing

In our story, one of Tomas Halle's problems is that he's been drilled into thinking that sticking to a pre-prepared media briefing is the best way to come away unscathed from the Committee chair's questioning. However, by depending on this script, and if anything being "over-prepared", he ends up spouting jargon and comes across as evasive and hopelessly inauthentic. Halle is also on the back foot because he's been told not to admit to anything, for fear of attracting litigation.

In fact it's a depressingly familiar performance: that of the CEO who's struggling to be the face of an organization in the teeth of hostile media questioning. Yet coming across as miserably insincere. Values not only need to be authentic, they need to be authentically expressed.

The interesting thing is that it's not a coincidence a large proportion of CEOs are poor in front of the media. It's because most of the world's CEOs are introverts.

This may strike you as odd, since extrovert CEOs such as Ratner, O'Leary and Diamond steal the limelight. However according to research carried out by a number of different leading organizations, boards and shareholders are much more likely to appoint introverts because they're seen as a safe pair of hands.

Francesco Gino is Professor at Harvard Business School, and a faculty affiliate of the Behavioral Insights Group at Harvard Kennedy School.** He explains that: "Introverts typically dislike noise, interruptions, and big group settings. They instead tend to prefer quiet solitude, time to think

---

* Published in mid January 2017 an Ipsos US domestic study for Buzzfeed showed trust in social media diminishes with age 14% 18–34, 12% 35–54, 5% 55+ www.ipsos-na.com/download/pr.aspx?id=16354

** Gino is the author of *Sidetracked: Why Our Decisions Get Derailed, and How We Can Stick to the Plan* (Gino, 2013)

before speaking (or acting), and building relationships and trust one-on-one."[18]

Glenn Mead, a psychologist who works at the company behind the bestselling Chimp Paradox theory, explained to me that introverts go on what they think rather than what they feel. All introverts are not the same but they tend to be deliberative, make careful calculations and are liable to analyse and think about the rules before making decisions.

In other words, introverts have a lot of what it takes to run an organization successfully, but communication is an Achilles heel. Extroverts work much more through their intuition, using automatic responses and associations based on images and experiences to make judgements. They come over as more genuine. Introverts revert to a script and come across as false. Having said this, among the many CEOs and senior managers I have worked with, it is the introverts—the quiet engineers, accountants and lawyers—who I have had the greatest respect for. Often saying not a lot but saying the right thing counts most.

I make this point at length because reaching and connecting with an audience is a massive challenge that few master. In this world of screens where the things we see and hear override what we read it's a challenge leaders need to deal with if people are going to follow them. It's fine having values but a leader who can't communicate why they matter in a compelling manner is potentially a barrier to success.

The 2016 Edelman Trust Barometer set out what people today expect from business leaders:

- Integrity is seen as the most important leadership attribute. The general population wanted to see leaders—in order of importance:
  1   take responsible actions in a crisis
  2   exhibit highly ethical behaviors
  3   behave in a way that is transparent.
- Eighty per cent of the population thought that CEOs should be personally visible in discussing societal issues.
- Nearly as many—79%—said that a CEO's personal values matter.
- Business leaders should have purpose. This should include: being dedicated to protecting and improving the environment; ensuring that the company creates programmes that positively impact its community; ensuring that the company addresses society's needs in its everyday business; and ensuring that the company partners with NGOs, government and third parties to address societal issues.[19]

One year later, the 2017 survey painted a bleak picture of deteriorating trust. It labelled 2016/17 a year that threw trust into crisis.[20] Restoring belief in a system that many people believe has failed, Edelman said, means businesses must operate as people-centric entities; an integrated function of the part of the broader social fabric.

When values get lost, it can lead to catastrophe. But more than avoiding the negative, values promote the positive. They underpin the success of a Single Organizing Idea. If people don't feel that the SOI embodies "good" values, they won't go with it. The values are there to help people live the change—it's something they can get behind and believe in. To paraphrase leadership expert Simon Sinek,* an SOI-driven organization is one where people show up for work for the same reason, and work together to achieve something they believe in.

In a global workplace where, according to Gallup only an estimated 13% of employees are actively engaged in helping their business move forward,** values are changing and the value of values has never been higher. They can help deliver experiences that align with and express the overriding purpose of the business and help engage and animate the most powerful advocates of the business, its employees.

In conclusion, I'll leave you with another thought from Gary Hamel's book, *What Matters Now* which captures the importance of values to today's businesses:

"An uplifting sense of purpose is more than an impetus for individual accomplishment, it's a necessary insurance policy against expediency and impropriety. By definition every organization is 'values driven'. The only question is, what values are in the driving seat?"[21]

---

* From the B Team New Ways of Working Report
** Gallup data gathered in 2011 and 2012 from nearly 230,000 full-time and part-time employees in 142 countries

4   The surge of technology

Stem cells to Star Wars

Hungrily feeding off the fresh science and engineering talent coming out of Cambridge University is an ecosystem of hyper-connected enterprises whose shared purpose is to shape tomorrow's world.

Some of the hottest tech businesses on the planet are located in what is dubbed "Silicon Fen". ARM, Apple, Amazon, Microsoft Research Labs, Raspberry Pi, Darktrace and Philips rub shoulders with giants from the pharmaceutical sector AstraZeneca, GSK, Pfizer as well as biotech businesses nurtured to success in the Cambridge area such Abcam, Horizon Discovery and Congenica, founded on the pioneering research from the world-renowned Wellcome Trust Sanger Institute.

In the gaps between these giants, thousands of "spin-out" businesses and "start-up" enterprises are being nurtured in state-of-the-art incubators and "seeding labs". The whole place is fizzing with ideas and possibilities. People with three brains, as one local described them, are busy making the impossible, possible.

Collis3Design is one such enterprise. Its base couldn't exactly be described as state-of-the-art. In fact it operates from the back room of a modest 1980s detached house on the outskirts of Cambridge, but the three brains description does fit.

Dr Elizabeth Hill graduated with a first class degree in chemistry, then built her own scientific instruments for her PhD research. Her work requires a top level understanding of coding, design, materials and testing. A self-confessed "techno-geek" she knows the Cambridge technology hub like the back of her hand, having worked on numerous due diligence projects for global financial institutions with interests in the healthcare and technology sector.

Her husband and business co-founder, Dr Howard Hill, also has a doctorate in chemistry. For many years he worked for the UK's Ministry of Defence as a specialist scientist on projects that can't be discussed here.

The idea behind Collis3Design is a truly exciting one. It is to enrich and inspire the next generation of designers, engineers and filmmakers. By engaging school children in storyboarding, designing and making, the pair aim to encourage schools to embrace 3D printing technology as a learning tool that advances their students' knowledge of science, engineering and art at the same time.

3D printing has been described by some as the catalyst that will bring about the next industrial revolution. In her presentation on the technology's potential, Elizabeth describes how in the very near future these quietly humming robots will invade our daily lives—and how they are already being employed in everything from stem cell research to Star Wars. Collis3Design's first product range is branded Minifigs Battlefields. Using free open source 3D software Howard has created blueprints for a host of world war one (WW1) objects that can be printed and used together with Lego® bricks to recreate key events from the war.

With pieces supplied by the business, school children learn about history, design, technology, storytelling, video, photography, sound and editing, and—importantly—teamwork.

Within a week of launching its website in June 2015, internet-based LUGs (Lego User Groups) frequented by AFOLs (Adult Fans of Lego®) emerged from across the globe eager to get their hands on the pieces, at literally any financial cost.

One of the first orders the business received came from a history teacher based in a school in Australia. It takes two hours to 3D print 10 French WW1 kepis (military hats). A trench ladder takes 30 minutes, barbed wire a little longer and the separate parts that make up a heavy British 18-pounder field gun take several hours. The Australian order was so large that it took two weeks to complete.

The rapid advance of technologies such as 3D printing brings greater efficiency, convenience and accessibility. Burgeoning advances like automation, robotics and artificial intelligence are fuelling our creativity and innovation and leading to a safer, more comfortable, more enjoyable and possibly more sustainable world. For businesses like Collis3Design that are determined to help change the world, technology provides an instant means of making a difference at scale in a very short space of time. Here is a prime example of a small business with a Single Organizing Idea at its core—to employ robotics and communications technology to advance education globally.

That said, technology is also a challenge. It is radically disrupting our world, and our growing dependency on it is presenting daily dilemmas. For example, millions of jobs that currently done by humans will be taken over by machines—think of the impact of driverless vehicles on every taxi, bus, van and lorry driver. In a short space of time many of the things that used to be a job won't be done by a human any more. And this is across the board. In many sectors technology-driven automation is commoditising traditional offers and devaluing any human involvement. Even people like lawyers are finding—to their dismay—that artificial intelligence (AI) can do a lot of the things that they thought could only be done by people.

It follows that organizations are struggling to come to terms with new technology. All too often those with a vested interest in the way things are done now use "deny, delay and disrupt" tactics to slow down the advance of the new. But that won't work long term.

In this chapter I want to demonstrate in particular the impact of new communications technology on businesses that are having to cope with the connectivity of empowered audiences of all types (staff, customers, shareholders and the general public). Increasing demands for freedom of information, greater transparency, speedier reactions to issues and instant gratification are among the challenges that businesses are struggling to keep up with, as we will see.

You broke my guitar dude

United Airlines damaged Dave Carroll's guitar. He saw them damage it from his seat overlooking the baggage handlers who were hurling luggage with abandon into the bowels of the plane. A professional musician, Carroll then endured nine months in "a customer service maze", as he put it, asking for compensation for the $3,500 guitar. Eventually, he got so frustrated that he wrote a catchy song—*United Breaks Guitars*—and posted it on YouTube.*

It's a great song and within a day, it was watched 150,000 times and within four days United Airlines' stock price fell 10%, costing shareholders about $180m in value.[1] Then, after nine months of stonewalling, United Airlines suddenly got in touch with Mr Carroll offering compensation. Oh, and they also had a small request—would he mind if they used his "excellent" video for training.

The video (which has now been seen by around 16m people) secured Carroll two top-of-the-range guitars for free and boosted his career. Along the way it has helped one of America's biggest airlines understand the meaning behind "positive customer experiences" a little better—not to mention the devastating power of the technology that we all carry around with us. One-nil to social media.**

Here's another example. In September 2015 several Zafira family tourer cars mysteriously burst into flames. General Motors' UK car manufacturer Vauxhall took no responsibility for the fires. They claimed the fires were "isolated thermal incidents".[2] Three outraged mums thought otherwise. Frustrated by the response from Vauxhall they did what people do today.

---

*   See: www.youtube.com/watch?v=5YGc4zOqozo
** Indeed, social media may have scored against United again in 2017 when a video of a man being forcibly removed from a flight was watched by millions of people, leading to the company apologising and offering to refund all the passengers on the flight, as well as review their procedures.

They set up a Facebook group to crowdsource and understand how big the issue actually was. Ultimately more than 13,000 people joined the group and around 200 fires were reported, from as far back as 2010.[3]

The growing social media heat caught the attention of mainstream media and coverage across newspapers and the BBC led Vauxhall to have a change of heart. Its chairman went on TV to tell the nation: "We fully understand the seriousness of the situation. We will not rest until we are fully confident that we have resolved this issue." The car giant promptly contacted 220,000 owners, offering them free inspections and repairs. Two-nil to social media.*

Then there's Monday 29th September 2014, a day Twitter user Chris Dodd is unlikely to forget. He was walking past a Sainsbury's supermarket on his way to work when he spotted a poster **not** designed to catch his attention. It featured the picture of a purse together with a 50p coin. Under the title "Fifty pence challenge" it read: "Let's encourage every customer to spend an additional 50p during each shopping trip between now and the year-end." Chris took a photo and sent it to @sainsburys. "Not sure this is supposed to be in your window," he said.

"Yeah, I don't think so either," was the swift reply. "Which store was this? I'll give them a call. Ross".

"Oh I'm not sure about that Ross…I kinda like that they're giving folks a heads up!" Chris replied.

"Understood. I'd really appreciate you letting me know which store though" Tweeted back Ross.

Poor Sainsbury's—Chris didn't tell them which store it was, the Twitter exchange went viral within hours and two days later rival German supermarket chain Lidl was running a poster campaign with a similar image encouraging "…every one of our lovely customers to save as many 50ps as possible." Three-nil to social media.

The lesson is that modern communications technology is an irresistible force that businesses ignore at their peril. It puts tools in everyone's hands that can bring hierarchies and organizations down. People can now outwit, undermine and expose businesses. Social media shifts the relationship and the balance of power between society and businesses of all types. Businesses are still struggling to get on board with that.

The trouble with social media

Here's just one of the issues: social media is a great leveller. It doesn't respect a person's rank or status. For instance, anyone can connect to and challenge a CEO through social media. Social media gives the people who are traditionally at the bottom of the pyramid a means of contributing their ideas and getting their voices heard.

---

* The Zafira's woes continued and in May 2016 the cars were recalled for a second time.

It's also a leveller because it creates online communities that operate laterally. Ideas flow across the community. They don't go up and down a hierarchy, being mediated at every stage.

For the older generation this takes some getting used to. If you've striven an entire career to get to the top, you may not be overly enthusiastic about any- and everyone having an equal say. You might see it as a threat, or an impertinence. Nevertheless, the technology that allows social media to thrive is replacing age-old practices and processes. For some it's empowering and for others it's actually the opposite.

Charles Arthur, a past technology editor at *The Guardian* and *The Independent* newspapers, said to me during an interview for this book:

"Social media represents both an opportunity, and a problem. Expertise and knowledge is not evenly distributed; but access to systems that allow people put their opinions forward is. Social media therefore elevates having an opinion over having expertise; and there's no simple way to distinguish whether an opinion is backed up by knowledge or is just an expression of feeling.

"That makes social media ideal for sampling opinion about, for example, a marketing message. How do people react to a new initiative? A new scheme? For some elements of those interactions, you want to be able to reach people immediately and hear what they say. People's reaction on the internet tends to be disinhibited, unconsidered and immediate—which can, if used carefully, pay rich rewards. But it isn't the place to rely on to get your reputation—corporate or personal—burnished. Nor is it the place where you should expect considered, expert analysis (though that can occur: some amateur sites provide remarkable in-depth examination of world events, marketing, advertising and science). Social media can be remarkable—but you have to be aware of its limitations before you begin to rely on it for anything."

In our story, the role of social media highlights generational differences. Tomas Halle for instance thinks that his indiscreet tweet is "only a private message on Twitter". Of course, he's wrong about this—he's sent out a public tweet. This is because he doesn't actually understand how to use the technology. Maybe he's intimidated by it. He didn't set up this Twitter feed, his PR chief did. Halle views technology with suspicion and caution. He feels like he's holding a snake that might turn round and bite him at any second.

Bibi, in contrast, is confident with technology and feels she knows how it can be used to best effect. After all, she's looking for funds to start operating a tech-enabled business. Moreover, she feels empowered by technology. It's connecting her to the world and giving her a voice and enabling her to pursue her purpose. It gives her a channel through which she can influence things and change them for the better. Technology is her servant. It's helping her realize her dreams.

What's more, like every young person, she questions things and wants to change them. This has always been the case but what social media does for her generation is allow them to put their stamp on the world in a way no other generation has ever been able to do before.

Tomas Halle is a Baby Boomer (born approximately between the years 1946 and 1964). According to research published in January 2015 by The B Team, Baby Boomers:

- Want to be rewarded for long hours
- Want authority to make decisions
- Feel work/ life balance is important
- Value social responsibility, and
- Want personal development opportunities in organizations.

By contrast, Bibi Okira is a Gen Y/Millennial. Individuals within this group:

- Value empowerment to get things done
- Want challenging work, collaboration, teamwork and fun, and responsibility for their own personal development
- Feel that the distinction between work and life is blurred
- Feel benefits packages don't meet their needs
- Like to participate in and contribute talent to communities
- Don't understand the concept of a career ladder
- Want constant feedback and instant gratification
- Mostly have been with their current employer less than three years
- Want to start their own businesses.[4]

So communications technology suits the freewheeling habits and aspirations of Millennials much better than the hierarchical, structure-loving Baby Boomers.

A generational difference worth noting is that Boomers think that the all-pervasive nature of technology is a negative. That it means they are always at work, "always on". Bibi, in contrast, as a typical Millennial, recognizes the crossover between work and play that communications technology affords her.

She would agree with the Institute for the Future which argues that rather than being "always on", workers can use technology to work more productively and achieve more in shorter timeframes. The Institute's *The Future of Work* report highlights how technology can set people free "from many of the fixed time, location, and work flow constraints that typify a traditional job. Mobile digital networks and collaboration software can help individuals create a better flow between work and everyday life—ideally enabling anyone to 'escape the 9–5, live anywhere, and outsource your life'."[5]

Communications technology also suits the smart companies that are embracing the opportunities presented, and tapping into people's willingness to get involved. Clued-in organizations use social media to ask questions, crowdsource ideas and get market-rich data, to spark innovation, increase customer satisfaction, heighten brand recognition and improve reputations. Used well it can generate revenue through successful online campaigns and be a powerful means of competitive differentiation.

Communications technology also enables organizations to collaborate, bring minds together and simply ask for ideas. Think of Apple, which created a platform to allow all-comers to develop apps. It led to an explosion of creativity. More than 100,000 apps were created within the first 18 months and Apple's rivals were left standing in its dust.

No place to hide

Another significant change brought on by social media is that it forces transparency. We live in an age of super-scrutiny. Businesses can no longer keep things hidden, try as they might. Activists and campaigning organizations make a point of finding things out and bringing them to everyone's attention.

It's also the case that what goes online stays online forever. Even where the 'original' of any Tweet or post is deleted, copies aren't. Content becomes indelible. Images on social media are extremely hard to erase. Researchers tested a range of sites to discover if photos could still be found online 30 days after their users deleted them. Seven sites, including Facebook, failed the deletion test, mainly because images tend to be stored remotely.

Savvy Millennials know this and understand that their digital reputation is searchable. Tomas Halle in our story needs to catch up because he seemed to think that deleting his unfortunate tweet will get rid of it. No such luck. Social media also had the capacity to pick his message up very quickly and very quickly amplify it with disastrous consequences, and there is nothing he can do to stop it.

Of course various government policies and regulations are being rolled out to support the "right to be forgotten". But in truth that will be hard to achieve because even many of the big content owners like Google hardly know themselves where the data goes. In many ways it's like gold—which is indestructible and can always be retrieved. When you delete something online you're just creating more data saying something has been deleted. Everything can come back to bite you.

Another facet is that communications technologies change the message. They drive people towards efficiency and speed—and messages that are often very short, streamlined and simplistic. The most popular social media channels are the ones that deliver quickly. Snap judgements, snap chats, likes, dislikes and emoticons with smiley faces and frowns are the language of the net. These short messages feel like shouts in an echo chamber—they get repeated over and over. There is little room for explanations or nuanced argument. Quite simply, people don't have the time. According to some observers these limitations are elevating hearsay and gossip to valid considered comment. On top of that, the Edelman Trust Barometer presented at Davos in January 2017 reported that nearly 60% of us now trust news delivered through search engines such as Google more than what is served up by human editors. According to the survey, 53% of us simply don't listen to news, to people or to organizations that don't agree with us, and today we are four times more likely to ignore information that doesn't fit or support what we believe.[6]

What does that do to the way people think? Bibi goes on Twitter to see what fellow-delegates are saying about the conference she's attending, but—as a typical Millennial—she's quickly diverted away to the Tomas Halle tweet debacle.

It's actually true that the attention span of readers is shrinking. The Pew Research Center conducted a study in 2014 which looked at the impact of living a so-called hyper-connected life. Results showed that such networked living drives a thirst for instant gratification and a lack of patience.[7] Social media is both a curse and a blessing, a cure and a poison. And that, in philosophical terms, is known as a "pharmakon".

Social media also changes and reshapes *what* people think. First it gives people a greater awareness and understanding of the world. So I'm buying a woollen jumper and the barcode on the label lets me find out how the sheep was treated. Or I'm buying a holiday and a large number of strangers influence my perception of a particular destination or hotel. Even though I don't know who these reviewers are, I still listen to them. (It's created a whole new industry where you pay third parties to write positive reviews about your product or service).

Then communications technology starts to homogenise people's opinions and their attitudes. I can give you an example of homogenised thinking from my own experience. I've run a particular workshop in 40 countries on five continents over the past two decades. I use techniques to help attendees describe how they feel about their organization now and how they would like it to look in the future. What they tell me is interesting, not least because across every culture and type of organization, people always say the same things:

- They always see a gap between now and then
- They always want better than now
- They always want to be modern and in-step with the world
- They always want satisfaction from what they do
- They're always surprised to be asked and appreciative that they were.

The other finding is that the older generation will tend to say that it's up to leaders to lead them, while younger people tend to be much more engaged.

They really think they have something to contribute and can make a difference. (This of course doesn't include young people who don't have the opportunity to attend workshops—the socially, economically or educationally excluded who feel disenfranchised, indifferent, powerless and apathetic).

And of course exposure to many different points of view raises questions about the received ways that things are done. It can coalesce myriad disparate points of view into a single, universally agreed version of the truth. It can spark demands for action and give them strength and momentum, as was seen in the 2011 Arab Spring where Facebook and Twitter are credited as having played a key role in galvanizing protests. The most popular Twitter hashtags in the Arab region in the first three months of 2011 were "Egypt", "Jan25", "Libya", "Bahrain" and "protest". Nearly nine in 10 Egyptians and Tunisians surveyed said they were using Facebook to organize protests or spread awareness about them. All but one of the protests called for on Facebook ended up coming to life on the streets. These and other findings from the *Arab Social Media Report* by the Dubai School of Government gives empirical heft to the conventional wisdom that Facebook and Twitter abetted if not enabled the historic region-wide uprisings of early 2011.[8]

Social media changes what people do and communications technology is literally changing the world. While the role of social media in the 2016 USA Presidential campaign is still being hotly debated, Donald Trump's digital director Brad Parscale put Trump's successful ascendency into the White House down to it: "Facebook and Twitter were the reason we won this thing. Twitter for Mr.Trump. And Facebook for fundraising" he told *Wired* magazine.[9]

The Arab Spring and the Occupy movement—which coordinated protests in 950 cities across the world—demonstrated an all-new capacity to spread ideas widely and quickly and to coordinate action via social media. Trump's online strategy raised $250m in campaign funding. It's a strategy he seems committed to pursuing, much to the dismay (and, in some quarters, amusement) of those that think Twitter is not the medium through which to govern the world's most powerful nation.

Listen to the man

Organizations need to rapidly adjust to the challenges that communications technology and social media bring. They need to accept the loss of control they once enjoyed and develop the capacity to listen, learn and adapt to a fast moving world that pits the pedlars of "fake news" and cynical "reputation management" agencies against the overwhelmingly genuine and honest needs and dreams of ordinary people.

Technology is just a vehicle. It's what you do with it that counts. The late Steve Jobs, CEO of Apple, put it like this: "Technology is nothing," he said. "What's important is that you have faith in people, that they're basically good and smart, and if you give them tools they'll do wonderful things with them."[10]

And that's the point. Now that people have a voice, they can and will be heard, and organizations need to not fight them on this—but to carefully listen instead. Communications technologies give organizations their listening tools. Businesses can mine the intelligence of their stakeholders, uncover insights and ultimately develop a strategy that people can buy into because they helped create it.

Do you remember a time when the CEO and his management team went on retreat on a wet Wednesday to write the organization's next five-year strategy? Those days are coming to an end, and rightly so.

They did this, by the way, because they thought that's what they're being paid to do. I argue that the flaw in this approach lies in getting people— employees and other stakeholders—to get on board with what they come up with in the first place.

In redefining IBM's purpose shortly after taking over in 2003, CEO Sam Palmisano harnessed technology to launch an interactive "values jam" that engaged 440,000 employees across 170 countries over 72 hours. According to IBM's Icons of Progress the values that came out of the process "Although created in a very new way, for a very new world, they are strikingly familiar—in keeping with the tone set by Watson Sr. in 1914"[11] (Watson was the CEO brought in to run "a messy conglomerate that would eventually become IBM". His first act was to preach the unity of purpose).

As Palmisano demonstrated more than a decade ago, communication technologies provide a powerful and different means to hold a mirror up to a business and see what it does, how it does it and for what purpose. To uncover some critical truths. As I will show in part three of this book, technology has become a vital tool. Not least because it helps bring people together to identify, define and nurture a Single Organizing Idea that they can all own as a united entity.

5 The rise of reputation and the fall of brand

Where's Wally?

I liked the way he looked. With his bowtie and round, thick-framed, goggle glasses he seemed like the professor of image that he was. But more, I liked the way he sounded. He was direct, clear and sincere. His "art" had made him a master of simplicity and in a sense that is what I think lay at the heart of what he stood for. I liked Wally Olins way before I ever met him.

In 1998 in a nondescript boardroom, so the story goes, Wally had spent the best part of an hour explaining how a goldfish would catapult FTSE 100 corporate Centrica into a brand new market. The "suits" on the other side of the table were having none of it and batted away each benefit behind the big idea as it was explained to them. Exasperated, Wally stood up, screwed the presentation into a tight ball and as he threw it into the bin and left the room said "I don't know anyone who doesn't like goldfish."

I can't imagine that anyone said "Where's Wally" but at some point he was called back and the Goldfish Credit Card became the corporation's first act in a diversification strategy.

Wally was a pioneer of corporate identity and the creative brains behind many famous global brands. During his 50-year career he was an advisor to many of the world's leading companies. Household names such as Tata, Renault, Volkswagen, BT, 3i, AkzoNobel, McKinsey and Fujitsu all sought his advice. At the turn of the last century I sought his counsel on a couple of occasions when I worked on branding programs for Merrill Lynch, Standard Chartered Bank, Novo Nordisk and Centrica's sibling BG Group. *The Financial Times* described him as "the world's leading practitioner of branding and identity."[1]

He wrote seven books on the subject but was never sentimental about brand, and certainly not the pseudo-science that has been built around the word over the past two decades. In his fifth book he wrote, "We should remain quite clear that what marketing, branding and all the rest of it are about is persuading, seducing and attempting to manipulate people into buying products and services." He added "…brands exist because they are a powerful tool that helps companies make money. And we the customers in the richer parts of the world know it. Nobody is really kidding anyone."[2]

Olins made it clear that brand is an orchestrated distortion, maybe even a kind of lie. In this he shares the thinking of social activist Naomi Klein, who in her 1999 book *No Logo*, accused corporations of hiding behind brands and using the power of them to encourage people to buy products they don't need at the expense of society and the planet.[3]

In this chapter I want to describe how the importance of brand is giving way to the importance of reputation. And how, in a competition between brand and reputation, reputation is going to win. But let's first look at what branding is.

A dark art

Branding is extraordinarily powerful. Brands tap into our minds and the best touch our hearts too. Brand masters bring together a carefully concocted alchemy of messages, symbols, sounds, tastes and even sometimes smells to create experiences that will entice us to buy. Their ability to position themselves in our consciousness and influence our decisions makes them critical to business success. Without them there simply would be no business. As the founding father of positioning theory Jack Trout said: "Out of all the different functions a business has, selling and marketing is the most important"[4]. Brand is central to both.

Sometimes brands are subtle but often they're not. Brands in general shout at us, they interrupt us and they badger us for our attention. Banks claiming to be the friendliest, internet hosts the fastest, supermarkets the cheapest, TV's the brightest, smartphones the slimmest, cereals the tastiest, water the purest, delivery companies the fastest and recently car manufacturers the greenest—it goes on, and on. Their demand for our attention is permanently "on-send" and everywhere we are, digitally stalking us and striking when they think we may be in the mood. Brands do help us make choices and where the products and services of competing companies are almost identical, brands do help us make decisions, often in ways that delight, entertain or comfort us. But that is their limit. Their *raison d'être* does not go beyond that. Brands don't care and they don't have empathy.

Brands are a conduit through which businesses, NGOs, places, governments and celebrities make promises. But it's not what the promises are that is leading to the inevitable downfall of brand. Nor is it the fact that we can no longer tell the difference between one promise and another—all smartphones are slim. Rather, it's our ability, curiosity and growing desire to look beyond the promises that is undermining them.

Brands are an impression of reality. The so-called "princes of darkness"* that create them and the spin-doctors that market them select, "buffet-style", bits and pieces of a business's DNA to mix a minestrone soup of fact and fiction. In our story, Tomas Halle believes that his Communications Director, Eve Grainger, has this power. All he has to do is stick to the script she has concocted and the lines she has fed him and everything will be okay. Unfortunately for Halle brand no longer has the power it did and the question people are asking is "Who are you really?"

The "suits" Wally presented to at Centrica were nervous about what they were being shown. In 1998, brand thinking was relatively new, and the nuanced complexities of the concept would have been totally alien to them as leaders of a gas distribution business. Fundamentally what they wanted to know was "Will it work?" In today's world, CEOs and senior management have a much greater understanding of brand—it's a subject that has infiltrated business schools and business thinking across the globe—but they have an even greater need to be nervous. Not only do they need to know "Will it work?" they also need to seriously consider "Is it true?"

The gorilla's lipstick has run out

Still today, all too often, the excitement of a creative opportunity, and the desire to deliver something fresh, vibrant or just different overrides banal reality and results in the building of a brand that is totally at odds with the business itself.

The consequences of this image-led thinking creates disconnects that can be damaging both internally and externally. For example, cynical staff trained to "live the brand" often don't believe in what they are being asked to help sell which in turn creates frustration among wary customers wondering what they are really getting.

Reputation, on the other hand, is **our** own estimation of that business and how we would describe it to others. As leadership coach Kevin Murray points out in his book, *The Language of Leaders*, "You cannot manage reputation. Reputation is a consequence of what you do, how you engage with people and then what they say about you."[5]

Though Halle seems oblivious to it, ours is an age of transparency, so his awkward evasions in the story are jarring. In fact in this type of situation the only reliable defence is the truth. And if that truth is unpalatable, there is nothing that he can do to hide it. Attempting to "live the brand" or in his case hide behind a CSR mask, just makes things worse. It is interesting to note that in a 2015 Ipsos public opinion survey of 18,531 people in 26 countries in June 2016, only 39% of people trust that CEOs tell the truth

---

*   The Executive Creative Director of a global advertising agency once described himself to me as the prince of darkness.

when they make statements about their company or industry (trust in CEOs is lowest in Great Britain (23%) and highest in China (71%)).[6] This strongly suggests that on-brand messages are getting in the way of truth. When you take into account that in Edelman's 2016 Trust Barometer, published six months earlier, 79% said that a CEO's personal values matter,[7] the power of brand as a defensive shield is looking increasingly unreliable.

What influences our perception is not only brand image—tone of voice and the way something looks and feels—but also ultimately the way it behaves and the way it performs. It is our experiences of these three factors—image, behaviour and performance—that combine to help us form a judgement of a business. And judgement is the right word because that is what we do—we judge, we rank and we rate.

What is important to understand is that today, in our hyper-connected world, while we may get some satisfaction from a story well told, beautifully executed packaging design, a sponsored event or a funny advertisement, we are no longer seduced as easily as we were. The curious minority of blogging renegades, challengers and mavericks have been joined by a technology-enabled mainstream of gossiping consumers and populist journalists looking for "info-tainment" pieces, all a mouse-click away from finding out things beyond the brand mask and dispensing what they find with attached warnings. Social media has engaged a new generation of nosey "scrutineers" and gossips. Technology has equipped them with the tools not just to ask questions but to find out the answers for themselves and then tell everyone else what they think. The brand carpet has been lifted up in many of our traditional institutions and the reality is being exposed. Everything is up for discussion—including the way businesses make profits, governments make decisions, and NGOs and faith-based organizations raise funds and influence self-serving outcomes.

While the power of brands remains potent, our goodwill towards them has been seriously diluted. Businesses build up "goodwill" with their customers over time and this can be cashed in, at the time of a disaster or mistake. Virgin, for example, has a lot of goodwill. We're prepared to forgive Richard Branson more quickly because he is perceived to be open and honest by the majority of people. When one of his trains came off the tracks in Britain's Lake District in 2007, killing one person and injuring 22 others, he was quickly on the scene and quick to apologize (yet it transpired that it was Network Rail's fault—a track inspector working for the track infrastructure business had failed to do his job). In the opening sequence of his 2008 gangster movie *RocknRolla*, director Guy Richie describes a "rocknrolla" as someone who has "got the lot"—sex, drugs and money. Branson is a "rocknrolla" of the business world and he's got the lot—image, behavior and performance. Which means that, while not untouched by controversy,* even in "tainted sectors" such as finance and transport he has been able to operate and thrive.

On the other hand, FuelGlow's poor reputation is compounded by the fact that the reputation of the energy sector is not overwhelmingly positive. In 2016 Edelman reported that only 47% of people in Europe said that they trusted energy utility businesses.[8] When trust is so fragile people are likely to condemn very quickly a business that steps out of line. In his case, Tomas Halle is calling upon a reserve of goodwill that simply doesn't exist, and we should note that in the wake of the financial crisis and the UK's horsemeat scandal that same well of tolerance and forgiveness has run dry for both banks and supermarkets.

Trying to remedy this mistrust with any kind of branding initiative, no matter how compelling the research and slick the agency presentation, is fraught with difficulty. Brands still matter but they don't matter anything like as much as the truth. The Ipsos Reputation Council, a group of representatives from some of the world's largest corporations, identifies authenticity as a quality that stakeholders feel is increasingly rare and greatly in demand. There is a significant advantage for those that can achieve alignment between communications and behaviour. A council member says, "If there is a dichotomy between what you say and what you do, you are going to have problems. So, in the end the messaging has to be authentic and the stories have to be authentic, and make sure that there isn't a gap between the rhetoric and the reality."[9]

Reputational reasons

In Chapter 1 I quoted part of the speech Paul Polman gave at the launch of Unilever's Sustainable Living Plan. He said "The more our products meet social needs and help people live sustainably, the more popular our brands will become and the more we will grow."**

In saying this he was setting out that a core purpose based on truth is the mechanism around which Unilever's brands will be organized. He was spelling out the purpose and the long-term intention of the business. He was setting out something the consumer could come to believe in, and asking short-term-minded "marketeers" and shareholders to believe in it.

Polman is asserting the authority of corporate leadership and corporate strategic intent to "do good" over brand management tactics to "do well".

---

* Naomi Klein, the Canadian social activist, said of Branson in her 2015 book *This Changes Everything*, "There will, no doubt, be more billionaire saviors who make splashy entrances, with more schemes to rebrand capitalism." p. 252.

** He's right, 'The Stengel 50 Index' shows businesses that share Unilever's philosophy and centered their brands on the ideal of improving people's lives resonate more with consumers and outperform their category competitors. www.jimstengel.com/grow/research-validation/

He's saying the former is more important than the latter. He's establishing a new philosophy and he's staking his and Unilever's reputation on it. He's put the Unilever name front and centre.

In the past Unilever was built on the success of a portfolio of individual brands. What has been behind the success of each one of these brands is masses of research, world-class innovation and superb creativity delivered over many years. One cannot underestimate Polman's ambition, nor his courage in challenging that formula. He has introduced a new model that puts in place a Single Organizing Idea, based on the truth, to ensure brands are not bigger than a shared purpose that aims to deliver common good. To achieve it he is leveraging the intent of the Sustainable Living Plan and getting the 170,000 people in his organization to understand that their shared purpose and their reputation is bigger than the individual brands.

So in changing the business he's asking which brands help or hinder the reputation of Unilever and its purpose. Dove and Lifebuoy soap both help. In fact corporate sustainability watchdogs often cite these brands, along with Ben & Jerry's, as trailblazers that are setting a benchmark for others to achieve.

But what of the other 400 brands in the stable? Which ones will help build Unilever's reputation and which have the potential to undermine it? This is key because, by definition, when you undermine the reputation of a business you undermine its ability to achieve its purpose. It doesn't mean that individual brands can't have their own distinct personalities, images, campaigns—they may even make different pledges to appeal to different types of customers. But they must align with the Single Organizing Idea to ensure they don't undermine the reputation. Pursuing this understanding helps ensure consistency, which in turn creates admiration and forges positive reputation. The relationship is complex but herein lays the link between reputation and purpose.

Unilever is in transition and will be in transition for some time to come. 2016 is year six of a ten-year plan. It's daunting but possible. Polman has redefined Unilever as Sam Palmisano has redefined IBM. Nike, too, has managed to almost completely redefine its business in recent years. Polman is asking the managers of his many brands to reimagine and reshape their brands to fit and help realise "A brighter future: A better business".

The end of spin

In reaching an understanding about how new thinking around brand and reputation is changing businesses, I was pleased to have the opportunity to meet Rupert Younger, the Director of The Centre for Corporate Reputation, an independent research centre established in 2008 within Oxford University's Saïd Business School. In a lively conversation, Rupert echoed the points made in a Harvard Business Review article written back in 2007 by Robert G. Eccles. The professor of management practice at Harvard

Business School wrote, "Firms with strong positive reputations attract better people. They are perceived as providing more value, which often allows them to charge a premium. Their customers are more loyal and buy broader ranges of products and services. Because the market believes that such companies will deliver sustained earnings and future growth, they have higher price-earnings multiples and market values and lower costs of capital." [10]

I will add that organizations with a strong positive reputation will be *admired*. You may well ask, why does it matter to be admired? Isn't being successful enough? Well my analysis is that it's better to be admired first and foremost than to be successful. This is because being admired brings sustained success. Merely being successful isn't quite enough today.

Oil companies and banks are extremely successful—in the sense that they make a lot of money—but they are not widely admired. The interesting thing is that most of them are putting in a great deal of effort at the moment to change that. And they're doing so because they recognize that, increasingly, consumers, staff and potential staff only want to be associated with companies that they, and perhaps even more importantly, their peers admire. Because they have a serious challenge on their hands when it comes to recruiting the next generation of bright young things. Remember, bright young things deliver new and better ways of doing everything. Without their ideas, businesses can't sustain success over the long term. If a business makes money and is also widely admired—that's the jackpot.

As we've seen, in our new age of transparency, how a business is regarded is critical to its success. It's something that cannot be purchased, commissioned or manufactured, but serves to drive future growth, innovation and prosperity. This is partly, as I said, because admired businesses attract the best people. But more immediately, in a world where products and services are essentially the same (functionally they deliver the same benefits: think about your car, phone, airline), reputation is the clincher. It's become the reason we select one version over another. It used to be that brand created the feelings that influenced our choice. But brands helped people make a choice based on a packaged promise made by the business. This is now less trusted.

What we've done instead is moved on from relying on what companies and politicians spin us through clever branding, to a model where we can, and do, find out for ourselves. So reputation helps us make choices instead. And because it's based on independent knowledge and experience, reputation is more believable. It's perceived as authentic and genuine. Brand, remember, is a kind of lie. Reputation is about the truth. Its only when Pinocchio stops the lies and becomes a "real boy" does he win lasting admiration.

Think about Soul House in our story. Across a wide range of activities— much like Virgin—Soul House seamlessly maintains a consistently high reputation. This doesn't happen because a brand is consistently applied across all of Soul House's activities (although it is, so that people recognize what does and doesn't belong to Soul House). It happens because consistency of tone, purpose, intent and execution comes from within—from the Single Organizing Idea that lies at the core of the Soul House business.

Meanwhile Virgin's Single Organizing Idea can be found in Richard Branson's 2013 book, *Screw Business as Usual.* In it he says, "Doing good can help improve your prospects, your profits and your business; and it can change the world. We must change the way we do business."[11]

Conrad is our Branson and Bibi is sold on this philosophy, as am I. She believes that putting an SOI at the core of your business, to drive profit and purpose authentically, is the way to go.

Soul House is also in transition. Just like Virgin and Unilever and all the other businesses that have decided that doing good is good for business. Conrad is building a portfolio of brands not just for the eco-minded but that all stakeholders can buy into. To do so, he's ensuring that Soul House is not just a name and the "back end" administrator managing resources and making efficiencies, but it's the visible "soul" of each brand. In the future I think we can expect to see many other businesses following the same course. Reputation-guided rather than brand-minded means that businesses can pursue a direction that brings them out of the shadows—so that when you see the brand, you see them.

Pinocchio stopped lying and became a real boy—those businesses that desire it and understand the value of reputation over brand can become real too. Businesses now have to find their Single Organizing Idea and live by it. Then reputation takes care of itself.

Reputation also creates legacy. Wally Olins CBE died in 2014. His reputation lives on.

6   Turning the dial

Okay, she said

On a cold and frosty morning in early February 2016 I called my friend Dr Andrew Moran at the London Metropolitan University. "Shifting Global Power" is the course Andrew runs and it includes aspects of international relations, peace and conflict, and diplomacy. I told him about the story I had created for the beginning of this book and asked whether he thought that his students would be interested in reading it and answering a few questions I had devised that we could debate. I hoped the answer would be yes. A couple of years earlier we had created a workshop together that allowed his students to play out the conflicting agendas of business, NGOs and government. It had been a resounding success and provided some fantastic insights into the way young people view the world.

A month after the call I arrived at the university. Andrew met me in reception and after negotiating our way through security's metal detectors we walked through a maze of corridors to his department. We opened the door to the classroom and sitting in the corner was a solitary individual too absorbed in her smartphone to even look up. It was five to ten and the session was meant to start on the hour. At ten just three others had joined our sole attendee. I began to worry that this wasn't going to be what I had hoped for. Andrew saw the look on my face. "These are students," he reminded me. "They'll be here."

Sure enough over the next ten minutes the noise in the room grew as more and more people arrived and took their seats. It was an extraordinary turnout and everyone who had received an invitation had turned up. Sitting in front of me, forty students had organized themselves into groups and were already chattering away about my story. With the exception of a couple of "mature students" these guys were all representatives of the Millennial generation and they hailed from right across the world: Somalia, Zambia, Afghanistan, Angola, Cambodia, DR Congo, Ethiopia, Nigeria, Mozambique, Romania, Estonia, Russia, Greece, Belgium, Finland, Germany, Spain, UK, Sweden, Holland, Grenada, Trinidad, Sao Tome and Principe, USA and Iraq were all represented.

During the next three hours I listened and made notes as they debated with youthful passion the questions I had presented them with:

1   Do you think the story is an accurate reflection of our times?
2   In the story, government is holding business to account. If we are not going to see the same state-led interventions in 15 years' time what needs to change?
3   The CEO and his communications advisor to defend his firm's reputation are using CSR. Is that okay?
4   The story symbolically contrasts two different geographic parts of the world, two different ways of thinking and the values of two different generations. Is technology and social media closing these gaps?
5   In the story it is suggested by Conrad James, the global entrepreneur, that business will always lack the incentive to pursue solutions that are good for society and the planet unless that imperative is built into the core of the business strategy. Do you agree or disagree?
6   Do you think that societal issues will eventually lead to changes to our market, trade and financial systems? Can capitalism evolve so that it doesn't compete with our planet but instead benefits it?

Their insights and points of reference were interesting in equal measure. Governments they see as largely reactionary and growingly incapable of keeping up with the rapid changes in the world and in particular the dilemmas technology is throwing up. They think that business models need to change to prioritize people and planet—and, interestingly, quality—before profit. They view companies that promote their businesses through CSR as cynical "trumpet blowers". Companies with good reputations and doing the right thing shouldn't need to boast about their achievements they say. They see Bibi as "one of their own" and share her ambitions and her modern outlook. But they worry about the impact of technology and don't think that it's necessarily the answer to everything. In particular they worry about who is in control of technology and social media and what is happening to data gathered by global corporations and governments. They cite *Adam Ruins Everything*, a television series that uses humour to challenge false impressions (described by the Washington Post as "well informed and witty") as being on the same wavelength as the story. John Oliver is another popular point of reference. He is an English satirist given free licence to entertain through the US TV show from HBO, *Last Week Tonight*, which regularly holds corporations to account. Oliver was included on the '100 Most Influential People' list published by *Time* magazine in 2015.

Interestingly, the students think that it is "ridiculous and unrealistic" that start-ups that have a grasp of the modern world are being undermined and held back by big corporations which want to control them and manipulate them so that they don't pose a threat to "the old establishment". The version of capitalism that Halle promotes and uses as an excuse to put profit before everything else is broken, they think. "Capitalism needs to evolve and adapt to a new way where cooperation makes the world go round, rather than money," they say.

Lunch beckoned after the debate but most of the students seemed keener to turn their smartphones back on than to eat anything. As they filed out of the room I shook hands and thanked each one of them for their time and thoughts. I was about to thank Andrew too when I noticed that the young woman who had been in the room when we arrived was still sitting in the same place. I went over to thank her.

"So, do you really think corporations will change so they can make a difference?" she said before I could open my mouth.

"Yes" I replied, "I know they can but it will be down to them defining their Single Organizing Idea."

"Okay" she said and without further ado left deep in thought. I smiled to myself. She reminded me of Bibi.

In the preceding chapters I've attempted to illustrate how our world and the way we work is changing fast. We've seen that while no clear alternative to capitalism is waiting in the wings, the capitalistic system is nevertheless under pressure to evolve into something different and it seems it is beginning to do so.

At the same time, traditional CSR is being challenged and is changing too. The Sustainable Development Goals (SDGs), a growing sense of urgency and new initiatives like Shared Value, B Corporation, Social Enterprise, Conscious Capitalism and the rest are beginning to focus minds and efforts. The pursuit of profit at the expense of society and our planet has become not only a question of sustainability but also of ethics. A new generation of technology-enabled individuals, like the students in Andrew Moran's class, have gathered around people and causes that continue to lay bare the inconsistent values and behaviour of some of our oldest institutions. Across the world the dynamics that we looked at are leading many to conclude that the case for change has become irresistible.

In the face of these changes, at the end of our story we see Mr Tang, President of FuelGlow's parent company, Halodi Holdings, undertake to set a new course for his global empire. Halodi's business interests are vast, as is the scale of his business, but Tang seems to be committed to the task. He certainly hasn't suddenly turned into a "do-gooder" but has registered that unless he changes, unless he responds to society's demands and the needs of the planet, he and his business will eventually fail. Witnessing the travails of FuelGlow confirms the insights presented to Tang following an independent analysis of his business. But sacking the old-school CEO and giving the green light to back Bibi's fledgling enterprise will seem like ad-hoc reactive, even cynical actions, unless the conglomerate makes good on its intention to put profit and social purpose at the very core of the business. A very real and concerted effort is involved.

With that in mind, and having established the case for change, in this final chapter of the second part of the book I want to build the case for the adoption of a Single Organizing Idea. I want to explain how your business can benefit from the power and potential of an SOI at the core of your business, and how, over time, it will result in actions that will help your business perform and compete better in the future.

The potency of purpose

In 2015, Cambridge University's world famous Judge Business School conducted research that showed that across 150 small and medium-sized businesses operating in "Silicon Fen", only half a dozen had defined their purpose.

Of the six who had defined their purpose not one single employee outside of the senior management team could state what it was. Had the scope of Judge's research been extended, it's possible they may eventually have found a business where everyone knew what its purpose was. But even knowing the purpose doesn't necessarily mean that people believe in the purpose, nor that they will all pull in the same direction to achieve it. It follows that businesses that are failing to fire on all cylinders are often falling short because many of the employees aren't clear what the aims and objectives of the business are—or they simply don't care.

It's a big problem that many managers I've spoken to acknowledge but seem powerless to put right—"It just is what it is", they say. And unfortunately the condition seems to be endemic. Gallup's 2013 *State of the Global Workplace* report on employee engagement found that worldwide only 13% of employees are engaged. It added: "The vast majority of employed people around the globe are "not engaged" or "actively disengaged" at work meaning they are emotionally disconnected from their workplaces and less likely to be productive."[1]

It's worth understanding why this is the case. To do so we need to very briefly turn to sociology. In the 1990s anthropologist and evolutionary psychologist Robin Dunbar arrived at a number—it was 150. Dunbar's Number, as it was to become known, was, he said, the maximum number of humans you would find naturally gathered in a functioning social group. Beyond that number of humans, unrest bubbles up and things begin to fall apart. In his 2000 bestselling book, *The Tipping Point*, journalist, author and speaker Malcolm Gladwell discussed Dunbar's Number and in particular the organizational experiments carried out by W.L. Gore and Associates, the firm behind the Gore-Tex brand.[2] But it is a much more recent book that got my attention. In his captivating 2011 book *Sapiens* Yuval Noah Harari points us towards religion, imperialism and mercantilism to explain what makes humankind different and what unites us, way beyond Dunbar's 150—and that is the potency of purpose, a shared belief: powerful Single Organizing Ideas.

Mission impossible

Of course many leaders and managers think that their purpose is enshrined in their business mission or vision statements. The problem is, however, that these terribly bland bromides have little impact on the consciousness of the business. The bottom line is that all too often mission statements are "pie in the sky". When the objective is to achieve world leadership status or similar, it is simply out of step with what the majority of employees want to achieve, or be associated with, or indeed find credible. People simply struggle to engage with these statements because they lack any kind of empathy.

Moreover, the posting of mission and vision statements and banal business values on office and factory walls makes them none the wiser. From business to business they're often the same: summoned up during a leadership away day and incorporating a clutch of interchangeable and overused buzzwords brought together to say not very much other than "we aim to be the best in our market". I can say with confidence that of all the organizations I have dealt with over the past 25 years, not a single manager or staff member has ever been able to recall the wording of a vision or mission statement, let alone understand what it means. The big picture is just not apparent to them and the fact that these meaningless directions come down from on high simply exacerbates a lack of motivation, morale and efficiency.

Of course that is not completely true.

Charles Ward is a semi-retired executive. Like many former senior managers who have completed a successful career, Charles is employing his experience to help guide others. I caught up with him not for his guidance but for his experience—a very specific experience from a long time ago when he was a corporate foot soldier. Way back in 1982 following three years cutting his teeth at 3M, Charles moved on to his second American multinational, the medical device manufacturer Johnson & Johnson as a product manager.

"The J&J credo was terribly important," Charles said. "They really meant it and for good reason—not only did it give the business purpose, it was the reason for its financial success." I asked what it said. Of course 36 years on he couldn't remember but one phrase had stuck in his mind "It was all about putting mothers and doctors first."

Later that day he sent me an email with a link to Johnson & Johnson's website. "I'd forgotten how long it was," he wrote. In truth, I'd seen it before but I read it again. Put "people first" I thought.

A crystal clear Single Organizing Idea that is defined to achieve profit and social purpose pinpoints and asserts what is truly important to the business, and describes exactly what it seeks to achieve, not just for itself but society at large.

Our Credo

We believe our first responsibility is to the doctors, nurses and patients, to mothers and fathers and all others who use our products and services. In meeting their needs everything we do must be of high quality. We must constantly strive to reduce our costs in order to maintain reasonable prices. Customers' orders must be serviced promptly and accurately. Our suppliers and distributors must have an opportunity to make a fair profit.

We are responsible to our employees, the men and women who work with us throughout the world. Everyone must be considered as an individual. We must respect their dignity and recognize their merit. They must have a sense of security in their jobs. Compensation must be fair and adequate, and working conditions clean, orderly and safe. We must be mindful of ways to help our employees fulfil their family responsibilities. Employees must feel free to make suggestions and complaints. There must be equal opportunity for employment, development and advancement for those qualified. We must provide competent management, and their actions must be just and ethical.

We are responsible to the communities in which we live and work and to the world community as well. We must be good citizens – support good works and charities and bear our fair share of taxes. We must encourage civic improvements and better health and education. We must maintain in good order the property we are privileged to use, protecting the environment and natural resources.

Our final responsibility is to our stockholders. Business must make a sound profit. We must experiment with new ideas. Research must be carried on, innovative programs developed and mistakes paid for. New equipment must be purchased, new facilities provided and new products launched. Reserves must be created to provide for adverse times. When we operate according to these principles, the stockholders should realize a fair return.

https://www.jnj.com/about-jnj/jnj-credo

Figure 5 Johnson & Johnson Credo

Let me give you three quite disparate case-study examples.

Hawkins

"Building Better Communities" is the SOI of Hawkins—New Zealand's second largest construction and infrastructure business. In a call to Geoff Hunt, Hawkins' CEO, I asked him what the impact of the SOI has been ten months after its launch. As you would expect from an understated Kiwi with over 30 years' experience running engineering and tech businesses around the world, Geoff is extremely practical and very down to earth. Over the 30-minute conversation he listed neatly, but totally "off the cuff" a series of tangible outcomes that have resulted directly and indirectly since the introduction of the SOI. In summary, the business is finding new ways to compete and grow that are delivering economic and social improvement.

For instance, a staff survey designed to take a pulse check on progress showed that the SOI has brought down internal barriers, begun to dismantle deep silos that had plagued the business and was forging a new sense of collaboration. Before the SOI, the majority of staff had felt disengaged. The post-SOI survey showed that this has been flipped on its head. Staff turnover has decreased and middle managers who had previously felt particularly cut off have become far more engaged, with some of them becoming active champions of a more socially conscious approach to business that is delivering positive financial outcomes.

Building Better Communities has also positively impacted on projects on the ground. Geoff relayed with pride how the thinking behind the SOI has helped frame and develop partnerships with government, NGOs and local communities in countries where the company has contracts. In Papua New Guinea, for instance, prioritizing local community employment, together with New Zealand-quality project management has resulted in the delivery of a highly profitable project that has lost no time to injuries and has created a huge sense of shared achievement. Nearly 25,000 people turned out to watch PNG's Prime Minister open the flyover that today serves as the gateway to the nation's capital Port Moresby. Back in New Zealand the SOI has helped galvanize conversations with national government that have resulted in an apprenticeship scheme providing indigenous Maori youth with a future trade and turned potential state beneficiaries into valuable state contributors.

"It's early days but overall the business just performs better," summarized Geoff. "Coupled with our new approach to seeking efficiencies and harnessing technology to ensure everyone is connected and enabled, the SOI is delivering real results."

There are plenty of challenges ahead for Hawkins, but right from the beginning the SOI had an impact. At the launch I was bowled over, as I always am, by the immediate response to what was being introduced. Following the speeches and a moving video that describe Hawkins' future as a business for good, an employee came up to me with the broadest of smiles on her face. "This is the reason I get out of bed in the morning—you've just captured it" she said. And that's all I had done—captured and defined it.

Most people I've met in businesses and other organizations relay to me the need to feel that they have a purpose and they're part of something that will give them satisfaction. Quite often that involves being committed to making a positive difference in one way or another. If businesses can harness, direct and "organize" around that desire and commitment through a "single" powerful "idea" that everyone can believe in and contribute to, then it truly has the potential to help change the world.

With the SOI in place, forward-thinking businesses like Hawkins and many of my other clients are at the beginning of an exciting new chapter in their history.

Volvo

Sweden's automobile manufacturer Volvo is a classic example of a business that has always had an SOI at its core. Though it may not refer to it as such, Volvo single-mindedly organizes everything it does around the idea of safety. Recently articulated through the marketing slogan "For Life", Volvo has a long track record of aligning what it does and how and why it does it with this SOI.

The business was founded in 1927 on the idea of delivering the safest car possible. The company went on to develop the three-point safety belt, pioneered child safety seating, developed impact protection technology and has been a leader in developing potential accident detection systems. In 2014 it launched "LifePaint", a special reflective paint that is invisible during the day and lights up in car headlights at night. So this is a car company that is looking after the safety of cyclists and pedestrians as well.

Volvo is a stellar example of a business that has employed an SOI to generate profit and at the same time benefit society. The pursuit of its SOI has driven it to develop breakthrough thinking, differentiated it from its competitors, ensured ongoing customer loyalty and earned it wide admiration. Without doubt, trends in the automotive sector and the positioning of competitors will have tested the resolve of Volvo's management to stick with its core purpose, but the SOI has endured. The bottom line is that the SOI is embedded in the business. Safety is a simple, sustainable and relevant idea that everyone understands inside and outside the business. On Volvo's website it states "Safety is part of our soul. Safety has been our guiding star since 1927." And actually, "guiding star" is a superb description of an SOI and what its role is. That safety has been Volvo's constant point of reference for the best part of a century is testament to an SOI's durability and proof of its continuing ability to deliver real results for both the business and society as a whole.

Community Clothing

Meanwhile, UK-based Community Clothing is not even a year old. I met the man behind it, Patrick Grant, in a soggy field in Pembrokeshire, south west Wales. Alongside 150 other brave souls that had pitched their tents in the rain and gale force wind, we were there to attend BFest. Organised by the hugely inspirational and energetic Andy Middleton of TYF Group (a sustainability education consultancy established over 30 years ago), together with the founders of the UK BCorp movement, the three day festival in September 2016 was a celebration of the first anniversary of BCorp's UK launch. I was there to research this book, and Patrick was there by invitation to understand the benefits his fledgling enterprise could gain from joining the BCorp movement. Somewhere in between the opportunity to "work, play and party together in the breath-taking Pembrokeshire landscape", we managed to find a quiet spot to talk about his hopes and aims for Community Clothing.

What immediately strikes you about Patrick, apart from his sartorial elegance, is his assured determination. It's a single-mindedness that has delivered him success both as a businessman and a fashion designer. In 2005 he took over and rejuvenated Saville Row's falling star Norton & Sons (est. 1821). Four years later he repeated the success and re-launched E Tautz & Sons (est. 1867) as a ready-to-wear line and a year after that in 2010 he won the Menswear Designer of the Year Award at the British Fashion Awards. But he is best known as the immaculately dressed judge on the television series *The Great British Sewing Bee*.

"Community Clothing is completely different from anything I've ever done before, or anyone has done before, and we are very much feeling our way forward," Patrick explained. "In essence it's a co-operative network and a commercially competitive fashion brand joined up via a societal purpose." The network part comprises of seven factories based in Scotland and the north of England that each share the same perennial off-season capacity challenges the fashion cycle presents them with. In simple terms, this is the "down time" that comes immediately after their high street retailing clients orders have been fulfilled. It's a time that spells seasonal layoffs and/or zero-hours contracts for their workers.

Patrick's simple idea is to fill this "down time" with the manufacture of high quality British-made clothes for his Community Clothing label. The Community Clothing brand translates the factories' outputs made during these "lulls" into a high quality "Made in Britain" value proposition that appeals to customers proud to wear British clothes made from premium fabrics sold at competitive prices. The start-up's range is small, cool and understated. A basic style of clothing that transcends being "trendy" and the like of which has made British fashion essentials famous—classic simple knits, selvedge-denim jeans, raincoats, pea coats and Harrington jackets.

With the brand having only been launched a couple of months before we met, the business case has yet to be proven but I was keen to learn more about its potential. In particular, I was eager to understand how people on the front line and outside the celebrity limelight Patrick is shining on the project felt about it. Lucy Clayton, Community Clothing's equally determined CEO duly obliged and on a clear, blue-sky day in late January 2017 I arrived in Blackburn, Lancashire to meet Dave O'Kane the Technical Development Manager of Cookson & Clegg, the factory whose plight had kick-started Patrick's idea in the first place. In an interview with *The Telegraph* that I read before my visit, Patrick set outs his motivation: "When I learnt that Cookson & Clegg, an E Tautz supplier, was on the brink of closure in 2015, I knew I had to take action. The idea of all that knowledge and talent being lost was heartbreaking. I knew and liked the people in the factory and I'd been working with them for years. But they were also making bloody important products for E Tautz, which we couldn't make anywhere else. So that April I bought Cookson & Clegg, paving the way for the launch of Community Clothing."[3]

Dave showed me around the factory. As we walked past the rails of Community Clothing pea coats and Harrington jackets he talked with pride about Cookson & Clegg's 160-year history and his own role in it since he arrived there in 1991 as an apprentice cutter. He talked about the backgrounds of the largely immigrant workers on the shop floor and compared their stories with his own as the son of Irish immigrants. His mother was a sewing machinist all her life and his father is still working "just down the road" as a cutter in a local denim factory. Standing on the gantry above the tat-tat noise of sewing machines he talked in plain language about the impact of globalisation and the loss of the hugely lucrative orders from the MOD that had been the lifeblood of the business but had gone to Asia. When he joined Cookson & Clegg it employed 140 people, two years later that was slashed down to 30 or 40 as a result of the business lost to Asian manufacturers. Desperate to survive, the business first turned to making workwear and "anything else we could find" before eventually ending up working in the uncertain world of fashion, manufacturing British-labelled clothing for the likes of M&S and John Lewis. "When Patrick stepped in with his idea he saved the factory from closure," says Dave. "He saved jobs but he also simultaneously secured his supply chain and that was clever. But best of all, in my mind, it's the sense of pride he's restored in us all. It not just pride in the clothes we're making but also the productivity levels we're achieving."

Following my visit I caught up with Patrick and Lucy again. Pride seemed to be the recurring theme of Community Clothing's short history, I suggested. "That's what lies right at the heart of it," Patrick agreed. "We both recognise that this is the core element around which all our stakeholders are gathering. We don't want to overstate it at the moment but that is what this is all about. It's a powerful essence that gives real meaning to our purpose."

It's interesting how things join up. Just a few miles from Blackburn stands the imposing form of Pendle Hill. It was on the top of this "great hill" that

A compelling, relevant SOI can be set at the core of almost any type of organization either in the public or private sector. But it must be based on the truth and it must be rigorously pursued and consistently delivered.

SOI	Type	Organization
Sustainable Living	Anglo/Dutch FMCG company	Unilever
Sustainable innovation	American apparel manufacturer	Nike
Partners for Good	American INGO	Global Communities
Collective Success	New Zealand tax collection technology	DataTorque
Safety	Swedish automotive company	Volvo
Promote and Protect	Global human rights organization	GANHRI
Smarter Planet	American business consultancy	IBM
Partnership	British high street retailer	John Lewis Partnership
Transformation	British environmental initiative	Eden Project
Commercial Success. Community Impact	British Regional transport business	HCT Group
Championing a better way	British consumer cooperative	The Cooperative Group
Mining the resource. Enriching the Nation	Anglo/African mining company	Debswana
Universal Accessibility	American technology company	Google
Assuring Confidence	American accreditation organization	ABET
Performance with Purpose	American FMCG company	PepsiCo
Ingenuity for life	German electronics company	Siemens
Networked Society	Swedish telecommunications equipment and services	Ericsson

Figure 6. Other examples of SOIs

- Combines your economic and social purpose into a single idea that sits at the core of your business
- Takes the potency of purpose and makes it into an organizing management tool
- Delivers absolute clarity which in turn builds consensus and commitment
- Aligns and ties together all your different contributions to society (see diagram 8)
- Attracts, motivates and unite staff
- Reduces costs through efficiencies
- Drives innovation
- Helps maintain long-term relationships with your stakeholders
- Multiplies the value of your business – fiscally and to society
- Reduces risks through meeting all stakeholders needs
- Delights customers by satisfying needs and expectations
- Makes your business fit for the future
- Enhances reputation
- Delivers competitive advantage
- Ensures growth/scale up planning is single-mindedly focused
- Makes your business first choice for customers, employees, investors and partners.

Figure 7 Benefits of an SOI

An SOI aligns and ties together the value of all your different contributions to society. Its single minded focus overcomes issues of nuance and duplication, and misunderstandings. It makes sense of the strategy which in turn builds consensus, generates commitment and attracts investment.

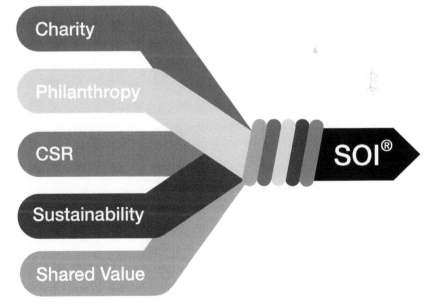

Figure 8 The potential of a Single Organizing Idea

lies "twixt Burnley and Clitheroe, Whalley and Colne"* that George Fox had an idea. It was an idea that subsequently led to the founding of the Quaker movement. I should know—I grew up in Colne.

Ten things an SOI can do—and four it can't

Hawkins, Volvo and Community Clothing belong to three very separate sectors yet regardless of this or the differences in their age, heritage, scale or location they are each organized around an SOI at their core that is helping guide them to sustainable commercial and societal success.

In conclusion, and before we get started on what it takes to put an SOI in place, here then is a final checklist of what an SOI can do for your business—and a few things it can't.

The top ten business benefits of an SOI

1   **An SOI empowers and engages employees**

An SOI generates pride. It unites people around a common cause and creates a shared sense of satisfaction. Businesses that invest in and fully commit to an SOI enable employees to build a high performance culture that thrives through everyone playing a role and being involved. The greatest advertisement for any business is the people who work for it. Having an SOI that empowers and involves staff will not only retain them but also attract others with ideas that share the same outlook on the purpose and potential of business.

2   **An SOI promotes flow**

Your business will perform better and operate more efficiently if it is organized around a single relevant and compelling idea. Alignment with a shared purpose demands a common understanding of the aim as well as an organized approach to achieve it. If we take an urban road system as a model, the sole aim is to maintain the steady movement of vehicles. Traffic lights serve a purpose in this respect, but they also encourage the stop/start behavior that ultimately slows things down. Roundabouts, on the other hand, maintain a steady flow. People get to their destinations on time, with reduced risk of tailbacks that impact on other parts of the road network. An SOI operates on a similar basis by encouraging every aspect of the organization to work towards the same aim. In many respects, much like the laws governing the use of a roundabout, an SOI provides the ground rules to build a modern, flat and decentralized business, that thrives on the confidence that greater efficiency and a free flow of ideas brings.

---

*   The chorus line of a local song about 'Old Pendle' I learnt at junior school. Its origins are not clear but if you're interested look up http://cliffhaslam.com/?page_id=308.

3 **An SOI attracts investment**
Authenticity is key to an SOI, and by extension the business as a whole. Businesses that define and align with a genuine SOI that takes it on a path of doing well out of doing good are increasingly attractive to institutional investors with an eye on long-term returns and the increasing number of "mom and pop" investors who care where their money goes.

4 **An SOI inspires innovation and promotes continuous improvement**
Your business may be well aware of plenty of opportunities being thrown up by a rapidly changing world but doesn't possess an organized approach to realizing them. An SOI enables the creation of an innovation mechanism that can engage the entire business in thinking about and implementing ideas. Importantly, innovation efforts that are guided by a single, compelling big idea ensure new, fresh ideas are focused and aligned with it. Innovation becomes a planned proactive activity that is geared towards the progress of the entire business and its cause rather than a reactive exercise that concentrates on individual functions of the business. In the process it opens the doors to new types of partners and new levels of collaboration beyond your existing network.

5 **An SOI breaks down silos and internal barriers**
When people work to realize a common objective, individuals and units within the organization learn to work more cooperatively and communicate more effectively with each other. Over time, long-held practices are refined and old-fashioned top-down control gives way to a state of shared stewardship. It takes time to challenge and break through patch protection and establish a new order, but an SOI is geared to guide and support the business through and beyond that transformation.

6 **An SOI delivers rewarding experiences**
Rewarding experiences are important drivers in the growth of any business. Meanwhile, every stakeholder needs to feel rewarded if they are to commit to the enterprise. With performance indicators in place, an SOI allows that experience to be measured, monitored, adjusted and evolved. It's worth noting that building report systems into the corporate calendar can optimize the effectiveness of this process. Evidence of progress and success are vital in terms of strengthening the organization, and can be easily communicated through every level.

7 **An SOI can set your business apart and give you competitive advantage**
By encouraging differentiation, an SOI effectively furnishes a competitive advantage. In many ways, this is a rewarding experience in its own right—and measurable, too, which further highlights the holistic qualities of SOI deployment.

8 **Adherence to an SOI builds a positive reputation**
Unlike so many business concepts, reputation isn't an invention. We can't create it like a brand, or bend it to meet specific needs. Instead, what we can do is assume *responsibility* for the way we are perceived,

and recognize that if we align every aspect of ourselves around an SOI then the impact will be far-reaching.

9 **An SOI makes a good business better (or great)**

It takes a business to the next level. If you're happy where you are then fine. But if you want to progress then an SOI can help to achieve just that. It serves as a constant source of inspiration for companies contemplating how they can develop, ensures continued relevance and sustainable success. A struggling business is one that can't find purpose. In this respect, an SOI is good for struggling businesses as much as those looking to improve their game.

10 **An SOI positions organizations for a sustainable future**

With an SOI in place, aligning the business to profit and social purpose, your business is able to make a valuable, unique and sustainable contribution to society. In effect, the outcomes that a CSR strategy hoped to achieve becomes central to the organization in *everything* it does.

This compels the organization to look outside for solutions, thereby enriching its knowledge and expanding its intelligence. It can also mean adoption of new thinking, processes, systems and innovations from outside sources.

What an SOI is not

1 **An SOI is not a marketing campaign**

We arrive at an SOI through a process of reduction that results in a succinct description of the purpose of the business. This is, of course, an attractive proposition to the marketing department, and there will be a temptation to draw the SOI into that sphere. It can inspire strap lines, as we have seen, but a note of caution is advised in externalizing the strategy. Essentially, an SOI is a valuable tool to be deployed within the heart of the business, and not simply pasted on the front of it.

2 **An SOI is not a radical way to run a business.**

This should come as a reassurance to some. It works, however, because everyone knows the purpose of the business. An SOI can achieve the same aim within a more traditional organizational structure. It doesn't require revolutionary thinking. It is, in fact, an *evolutionary* process in terms of deployment, requiring just clear-sightedness and commitment.

3 **An SOI is not something a business won't feel**

A business doesn't need to advertise the fact that it has adopted an SOI. The cohesion, drive and shared purpose generated by the framework creates an unmistakable vibe. A sense of camaraderie binds the entire entity. The SOI creates a unique environment that permeates and guides every aspect of the organization, from the style of leadership, the types of people it selects, the systems and processes it employs, to the products and services it delivers.

4   **Implementing an SOI is not a quick fix**
A good SOI is not merely an elegant proposition on paper. In reality, it's a powerful tool, but implementation takes courage, leadership and not a little patience. Leadership is critical here, and the right person needs to be driving the organization for the transition to be successfully achieved.

A powerful and sustainable SOI goes beyond the articulation of a purpose. It will guide your business over many years, regardless of changes to market trends, leadership and technology. It is the result of investment into inclusive inquiry, succinct definition and consistent and disciplined implementation. In the third and final part of book we will look at exactly how that is achieved.

Part 3

Changing for good

Introduction to part 3

Evidence shows that businesses that set out to create wealth and contribute to society in equal measure do well. They increase their competitiveness, achieve preference and solve issues. Hopefully I have demonstrated in the two preceding parts that a Single Organizing Idea (SOI) is valuable and has the power and potential to change your business for good.

Spurred on by COP21 in Paris and the ratification of the UN's Sustainable Development Goals in late 2015, forward-thinking companies are redefining their purpose and seizing the opportunity to make a positive difference and move ahead. In my opinion those that spectate run the risk of being left behind.

Changing a business for good requires not only defining or redefining the core purpose, but a change in how the business is organized so that the idea behind its purpose can be effectively managed and sustained. For any business this is a huge undertaking. It can't be approached in a piecemeal manner. Aside from the desire to change, identifying, defining and finally weaving an SOI into the fabric of your business requires courage, collaboration, commitment, hard work, time and investment. It's important to understand from the outset that to be successful, more than anything, it requires a structured and disciplined approach that everyone can believe in and contribute to. The third and final part of this book is about how to do that.

In the first three chapters of this final part, I set out my thoughts on the methods and approach that have helped me to identify, define and implement successful SOIs for organizations of all sizes and sectors, both for-profit and not for-profit. This process is illustrated in the figure below. There are no "closely-guarded secrets" to be revealed—in fact the process is based on common sense and practice, but change is complex and what looks good in theory often doesn't look so pretty in reality. So, in the final chapter I will lay bare some of the realities of the challenge. I hope it will benefit your business, but first, let me quickly tell you a bit more about the origins of those three letters—SOI.

The approach to defining, creating and then aligning business with an SOI doesn't need to be complicated but it does need to be logical, practical and inclusive at every stage.

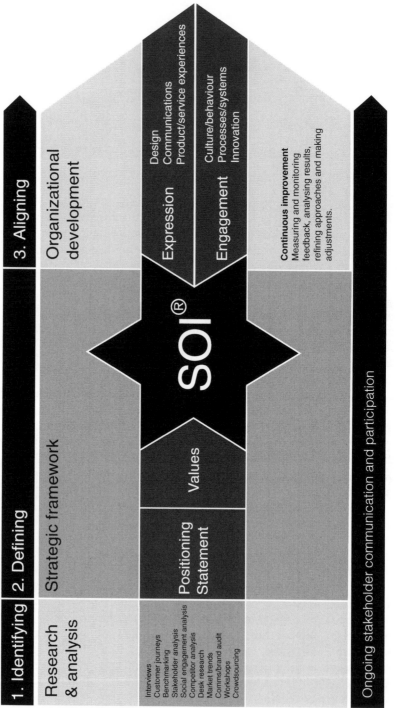

1. Identifying	2. Defining	3. Aligning
Research & analysis	Strategic framework	Organizational development

Positioning Statement

Values

SOI®

Expression
- Design
- Communications
- Product/service experiences

Engagement
- Culture/behaviour
- Processes/systems
- Innovation

Interviews
Customer journeys
Benchmarking
Stakeholder analysis
Social engagement analysis
Competitor analysis
Desk research
Market trends
Comms/brand audit
Workshops
Crowdsourcing

Continuous improvement
Measuring and monitoring feedback, analysing results, refining approaches and making adjustments.

Ongoing stakeholder communication and participation

Figure 9 The process of designing, creating and aligning an SOI

To be clear, I did not invent the term 'Single Organizing Idea'. It was actually coined by the 20th-century philosopher Isaiah Berlin. He co-opted an ancient Greek parable, *The Hedgehog and the Fox,* and used it to explain, in a famous essay of the same name, that there are two types of people: those like the fox that know many things, and others, like the hedgehog, that know only one really big thing.[1]

The key is that this is good for the hedgehog. Foxes pursue many ends at same time, and never integrate their thinking into one overall concept or unifying vision. The hedgehog, meanwhile, focuses on one important thing—which is maintaining impregnable defences against the fox. Consequently, when they battle, the hedgehog always wins.

In his 2001 bestseller, *Good to Great,* Jim Collins picked up this reference to the parable to help explain his 'Hedgehog Concept'.[2] Hedgehogs, he said, "simplify a complex world into a single organizing idea, a basic principle or concept that unifies and guides everything." This was Collins' passing reference to an SOI. He subsequently talks about "the power of the hedgehog", which he explains as: "a piercing insight that allows them to see though complexity and discern underlying patterns. Hedgehogs see what is essential and ignore the rest." This is where I first came across specific mention of a "single organizing idea", which I have developed to look like this:

The Single Organizing Idea (SOI)

Single

This expresses that it's crucial to have one purpose—and no more. We want a single-minded business focused on the pursuit of one shared purpose that everyone understands and can contribute to. The single purpose gives enduring and constant clarity no matter the many objectives a business needs to achieve and manage in its day-to-day operations.

Organizing

This describes the mechanism that governs, informs and marshals every function of the business to ensure the overriding purpose is achieved across the board. Discipline and tireless consistency cuts through silos and illuminates competing agendas.

Idea

This describes the concept that lies at the heart of the business. It is the reason for the existence of the business in the first place. All businesses start off with an idea, but they are fragile. The SOI ensures the idea is protected and maintained over the long term and has supremacy over all other ideas. So the purpose is more than a purpose. It's an idea—or an ideal—to be achieved.

Single Organizing Idea (SOI)	Values	Positioning statement

Figure 10 Strategic framework template

The strategic framework

The SOI is the lynchpin of a simple strategic framework that comprises just two other elements: values and a positioning statement.

Values

Simple words like safety, pride, promote, protect, assure and advance are powerful calls to action that make immediate sense, both logically and emotionally, as an SOI. But they don't describe how the action or aim can be achieved. This is where values come in. Values ensure that decisions, actions and behaviours support the SOI and ensure its consistent delivery.

When values are presented as passive, empty statements displayed on office reception walls, set out in promotional brochures or on websites, as they often are, they mean next to nothing. But as day-to-day drivers of unity, performance and accountability they become powerful influencers of positive outcomes that determine alignment with the SOI.

Positioning statement

The third and final component of the strategic framework is the positioning statement. This is a crucial element because it frames the context in which the idea—the single organizing idea—is operating and at the same time conveys the value or benefit of it.

The positioning statement is an explainer—it's the elevator pitch. It is two or three tailored sentences that can be delivered in 30 seconds, the objective of which is to convince the listener of the benefit of the idea. Indeed, it should not only convince but lodge in the mind. For that reason it needs to make two or three points that convey the energy and possibilities of the idea in such a way that they spark interest and a desire to know more. While

Johnson & Johnson's Credo is a fantastic statement it clearly doesn't fit this ideal—it's simply way too long. My humble suggestion would be that an updated version be drafted that includes reference to its heritage and the original be archived.

The positioning statement does not need to be repeated rote fashion. Rather its contents should be used to inspire and be adapted and refined depending upon who is delivering it and most importantly who is listening. It goes without saying that for it to be convincing it absolutely must be truthful and sincere.

7 Phase 1: Identifying

Doing your homework

Businesses need to achieve a clear-eyed understanding of where they are now before they can even begin to start thinking about a redefined purpose that will deliver good for all. Without understanding the truth about your business it is impossible to frame what degree of change is going to be required, and what stands in the way of change and the effective implementation of an SOI.

Understanding what makes your business valuable already—beyond the fiscal—is critical to future success, as is determining its culture and underlying values. The SOI will be the anchor point of your business over the long term. It will need to be sustained regardless of leadership changes, technology advances, market trends and socioeconomic developments. Anything less than a thorough and robust evaluation of the business and its context risks inviting issues and the kind of unintentional consequences we looked at in our story and in Part 2.

An SOI is discovered or uncovered and then defined—it is not made up. It is the result of looking and listening hard to what is going on both inside and outside the business. It requires that the right people be asked the right questions. Prodding and probing for insights and hard facts helps frame both the challenges and the opportunities. Ultimately it sorts out "what is" from "what could be" and it is equally important to consider the "identifying" phase as an opportunity for deep self-reflection, which shouldn't be entered into lightly.

To be successful the identifying phase should be approached with a completely open mind free of assumptions. This can only be achieved through the eyes of a third party and engaging a trusted or recommended independent consultant who is not connected to your business is essential to this kind of task. The consultant you choose should have skill and judgement, have a measured personal approach, have humility and at the same time be firm. A straight talker, he or she should be a future thinker but not an idealist; an "ideas" person who is able to weigh possibilities and opportunities against realities and practicalities. Instinct and intuition, discipline and diligence should propel them to collect and assimilate information from multiple sources and deliver a hypothesis based on informed intuition. Gerard Hodgkinson, author of *The Oxford Handbook of Organizational Decision Making*, helps describe the ideal candidate for the task. According to Hodgkinson, he or she should be equipped with a "broad constellation of past experiences, knowledge, skills, perceptions and feelings." Ideally they should work for an organization that has strategy as its main deliverable and, of course, doing good as their core purpose.[3]

What is **not** important is that he or she has a deep understanding of your business or the sector that it operates in. In fact, this lack of knowledge is an important advantage, especially during the first phase as they will challenge ideas and ask questions not normally asked. A combination of "fresh eyes" and a willingness to ask carefully crafted but perhaps "obvious questions" can reveal insights that can be overlooked by someone who has established knowledge and experience of your sector. Incumbents are likely to make assumptions more readily, take short cuts and miss opportunities.

It is critically important that leadership and staff are confident that the information gathered, the options presented and the recommendations made are derived from a fact-based and unbiased analysis of your business. Of course no amount of time spent on research and no amount of data can ever satisfy everyone and there has to be a cut-off point. But taking a practical approach will lead to key insights and ensure a satisfying return on your investment down the line.

In the first instance then, and before a hypothesis can be arrived at, three aspects of your business need to be examined and understood:

1   **Understanding the business:** what does it do? how does it make money? what are its objectives? how is it managed? who are its customers? who are its competitors? what do its operations look like?
2   **Understanding the stakeholders:** what is their influence? what are their needs, cares and wants? how diverse are they? who/what influences their opinion? how do they engage with the business?
3   **Understanding the social context:** what are the issues facing the business? in what way and where does the business impact on society? what sustainability or CSR initiatives are in place?

1 Understanding the business

Desk research

Desk research can paint a rich picture of the business and the environment in which it competes. It helps reveal how the business is positioned, what its objectives are and how it behaves and performs in pursuit of them. It also shows how the business itself wishes to be seen and how effectively it manages its image.

Understanding what your business does and the environment in which it competes can be gained from a wide variety of sources including strategy documents, annual reports, CSR reports, organization charts, marketing strategies and marketing materials, brand guidelines, HR policies, internal surveys, customer segmentation, press cuttings, events and online commentary from review sites. I often augment this desk material by asking for a tour and taking photos of the business environment(s). Interesting insights can be drawn from noticeboards, a reception desk that is permanently empty or even room naming solutions. It is the little things that augment the big things to create the overall impression and "vibe" of a business.

Competitor analysis

The future intentions and current positioning of competitors relative to your own business will help identify an SOI that lays the groundwork for competitive advantage. I am careful to say how competitors are positioned and not their strengths and weaknesses. While knowing how many people your competitors employ, what their product range is, what their history is, how much they spend on R&D, where they buy their materials and at what rate, is all of some interest, but what is most important is to understand how they create customers.

The objective of the competitor analysis is therefore to understand what methods and messages are being successfully employed to attract customers. By identifying the key marketing messages of competing businesses, the hard and soft qualities they use to attract custom and the consistency with which they do so through image and actions, it is possible to map their positioning.

Critically, because the objective of the SOI is to enable your business to contribute to society as well as create wealth, it is important to understand what kind of societal issues/CSR initiatives are being addressed by your competitors. I hasten to add that that is not necessarily so that you can avoid tackling the same cause or issues down the line. On the contrary, the greater opportunity is perhaps to partner and collaborate with your competitors in the way NGOs often do. In the building sector for instance there are a number of forward-thinking construction firms that see their purpose as being "building better communities". Infrastructure and construction company Hawkins, who we looked at in Chapter 6, shares a common purpose with its local rival Fulton Hogan in New Zealand and with Land Lease globally. In theory, if businesses were to partner more often on projects, their shared purpose and those that contribute to it could be organized to maximize impact and avoid duplication. That may be a lofty ambition, but it does happen and I am optimistic that it will happen more in the future as businesses develop their understanding of what is important and the power of a shared purpose.

Analysing and mapping how competitors position themselves in the market is a key requirement. Mapping not only highlights the espoused strengths of each competitor but also captures the degree of engagement with society. Is social engagement core to the purpose of the competitor (high) making it cause as well as financially driven or a tactical bolt-on being cosmetically applied (low)?

Personality	Approach	Offer	Presence
Relationships Understanding Interaction	Knowledge Expertise Processes	Innovation functions/options specifications	Scale Location/network History

Intangible → Tangible

Social engagement: High ↔ Low

Benchmarking

An external consultant with broad experience will bring knowledge from other sectors. Identifying and comparing best practice from other areas helps establish not only what is possible, but also how it might be achieved.

Benchmarking is a great way to mitigate risk. Investing time and effort in gathering success stories from other industry sectors not only provides reassurance but helps explain the advantages and challenges of change. Adopting or adapting what has been successful elsewhere can give comfort to those people in your business who are averse to or nervous of change. Of course, the benchmarking examples have to be relevant, but when you consider what the objective of identifying and defining an SOI is, you may be surprised how diverse those examples might be. A mixture of first-hand knowledge and researched successes and failures gathered from GE, Vodafone, IBM, Starbucks and Unilever helped me describe how initiatives and approaches in the private sector could be adopted or adapted to help one of the largest faith-based international NGOs on the planet understand its potential. Similarly, I have identified and presented case study examples that demonstrate the empathy of NGOs to help inform the views of leaders in private sector companies. It makes sense that, if businesses are to become more like NGOs and NGOs more like businesses, they learn from each other.

Touch-point analysis

Every business has touch points. Often referred to as "moments of truth" these are the times when people come into contact with your business. A touch-point analysis of people's experiences at these moments not only helps pinpoint where the business engages with stakeholders, but what their reaction is to your business at that time.

While it can sound like jargon, different types of people travel along different "touch-points journeys". For instance, an employee's journey will include their experiences as a job candidate, the environment they work in, the tools they are asked to use, interaction with others, internal communications, company rituals and policies, etc.

The experiences your stakeholders have at touch points will leave a lasting impression on them. These impressions are often "felt" and can range from feeling mildly or extremely negative or positive about your business, to being completely nonplussed. From these impressions or perceptions, individuals form a point of view and may take action as a result. For instance, if the experience is positive and resonates with their expectations, or even delights them in some way, it is likely that they will want to repeat it and they may encourage others to do so too. On the other hand, if the experience is negative the opposite is true—they won't want to repeat the experience and may even warn off others in their network. Our "fight or

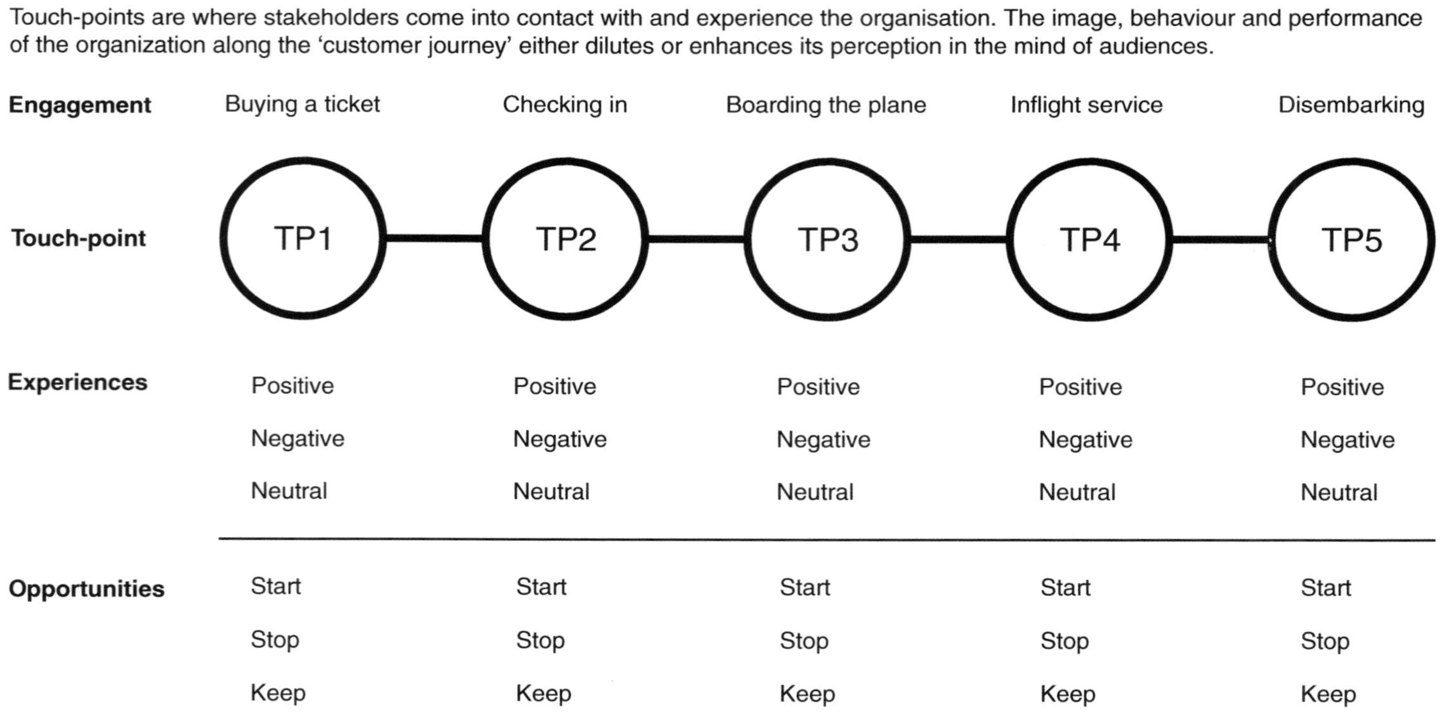

Touch-points are where stakeholders come into contact with and experience the organisation. The image, behaviour and performance of the organization along the 'customer journey' either dilutes or enhances its perception in the mind of audiences.

Engagement	Buying a ticket	Checking in	Boarding the plane	Inflight service	Disembarking
Touch-point	TP1	TP2	TP3	TP4	TP5
Experiences	Positive	Positive	Positive	Positive	Positive
	Negative	Negative	Negative	Negative	Negative
	Neutral	Neutral	Neutral	Neutral	Neutral
Opportunities	Start	Start	Start	Start	Start
	Stop	Stop	Stop	Stop	Stop
	Keep	Keep	Keep	Keep	Keep

Figure 12 Moments of truth of an airline business

flight" human response to experiences can trigger an instant reaction. As we saw in our story a mobile device literally at hand that has the potential to reach hundreds of thousands of people in seconds with an instant assessment of your business can be devastating.

Businesses that seek to repurpose around a cause need to carefully consider the impact of taking such a course, and do everything to ensure that stakeholder experiences of behaviour and performance at touch points are consistent with the organization's declared core purpose.

The relationship between a business and its stakeholders can be complex and it is worth bearing in mind that employees can also be customers and shareholders. By carefully and sensitively signposting your intentions, values and commitments at touch points it is possible to turn stakeholders into unpaid ambassadors whose messages are aligned with the Single Organizing Idea. This can be much more compelling than making grand declarations through external advertising for example. Smart feedback mechanisms at these touch points can also encourage people to get involved and their actions, ideas and communications can help further the business and give greater clarity to its cause.

2 Understanding the stakeholders

Stakeholder analysis

According to a 2004 report in the *Financial Times*, the definition of a stakeholder is "anyone who can bugger up your business."[4] Broadly speaking there are two types: primary and secondary. Primary stakeholders literally have a stake in your business and its economic success directly affects them. Shareholders, employees, customers, consumers, owners, creditors, investors, governments (tax collecting), suppliers, partners, contractors and local communities fall into this category. Secondary stakeholders are largely external. The actions and behaviours of the business can affect them and vice versa. They include unions, government (regulation/ policy making), trade associations, NGOs, advocacy groups, potential customers, potential employees, competitors, experts and analysts, education institutes, media, alumni, think tanks, researchers and the general public.

I set this list out at length because the variety of stakeholders is often a surprise to even the most experienced managers. It is also worth noting that within the context of defining an SOI that is to be employed for good, the planet itself is, of course, a substantial stakeholder. Even though it doesn't have a voice as such, nature and the climate can certainly bugger up your business in a major way!

Understanding your stakeholders' perceptions and their attitudes towards your business is vital. Without understanding what concerns them—what they need, want and care about—a business cannot define and organize itself around a purpose that has value to them.

Mapping stakeholders is an important part of identifying who your audiences are, what their perception of your business is and the degree of influence they have in shaping that perception. The number of stakeholders types can be large and their individual agendas often conflict.

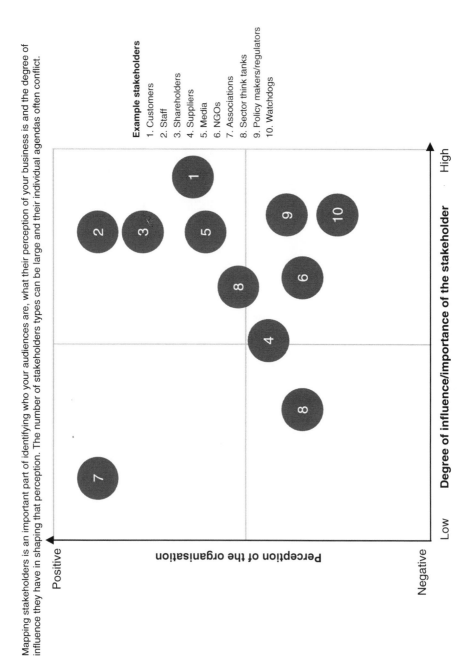

Example stakeholders
1. Customers
2. Staff
3. Shareholders
4. Suppliers
5. Media
6. NGOs
7. Associations
8. Sector think tanks
9. Policy makers/regulators
10. Watchdogs

Figure 13 Stakeholder matrix

Generally speaking, stakeholders form their opinion of your business either through their direct experience of your services or products (be they positive, negative or neutral); through media comment or through hearsay. As we have seen, hearsay or, if you like, gossip shared through social media channels can have an immediate impact and quickly change stakeholder opinion. As Charles Arthur indicated in Chapter 4, on the impact of technology, the increasing use of hieroglyphic "emoticons" to instantly rank and register likes and dislikes are superseding qualified insights and real investigation. The 2016 US Presidential campaign and Brexit are high profile examples that demonstrate a growing trend for condensing everything into social-media-friendly sound bites. Distortion and half-truths are readily mixed into a 24/7 news loop that increasingly seems to be geared more towards entertaining than informing. The bottom line is that what stakeholders think and feel about your business may not even be based on the truth, and their opinion maybe changed in an instant.

Interviews

For me, interviews held in confidence are the single most important element in any research programme and are the very best method for understanding what a business is really about. I have relied on them extensively in every engagement I've ever taken on and look forward to them eagerly. Interviews are the opportunity to look someone in the eye and uncover the truth about their business. They reveal the values, qualities and motivations upon which success depends. Just as importantly, they provide an opportunity to assess the qualities, values and motivations of the interviewees themselves.

A list of internal and external interviewees who represent a broad spectrum of opinion formers as well as decision makers is critical. Interviews should be prioritised in a logical order so that accumulated knowledge can be taken from one interview to the next. The CEO is naturally seen as the first port of call, but in many cases I have found it useful to talk to other people in the organization first.

Interviews are not surveys and need to be taken up on an individual basis with questions being developed and refined as the identifying phase progresses and knowledge is gathered and understood. As well as gathering facts, stories, thought and feelings, interviews present an ideal opportunity to test support for ideas and potential challenges or resistance to them.

Staff workshops

Workshops designed to mine the minds of employees for thoughts and ideas are also a fantastic vehicle through which change can be introduced and understood. In my experience staff are still very rarely called upon to share their thoughts and ideas. Some businesses do have innovation programmes and feedback mechanisms that engage their workforce from time to time but the vast majority don't. So staff are often surprised to be invited to a workshop that gives them a role beyond their day jobs.

I glean the thoughts and feelings of staff through a workshop format that has remained largely unchanged for almost 20 years. Regardless of the level of staff being engaged, the industry they work in or the country they live in (I have run it in over 40 countries), I have found that the most fruitful approach is an open one that's not intent on "selling" an ideal or reaching conclusions. Through listening and observing, it is possible to uncover important insights and, perhaps more importantly, the values necessary to underpin them. Setting a context based on reality and then running exercises that allow staff to express their concerns and aspirations as individuals, in teams and, finally, as an entire group can be extremely rewarding.

Like interviews, all workshops are different and some of them can be difficult. It is often said that most people are resistant to change and that resistance can sometimes be expressed even when the benefits of change are clear. But a well-structured workshop programme that is designed to take stock of what a group thinks and how they are feeling can quickly establish a sense of inclusion. If the results of the workshop materialise into a purpose they contributed to, it is much more likely that staff will believe in it and make suggestions that will make it a reality down the line. Of course the mechanisms need to be in place to allow that to happen and that is part of the implementation phase that will be covered later.

I just said it is common to be told that people are resistant to change. But perhaps it would be more accurate to say that some people are uncomfortable with change and almost all recognize the need for it. Without exception every workshop I have ever run has identified a gap between how staff perceive their business today and how they would ideally like to perceive it in the future. Sometimes that gap is small and sometimes it is large, but in every single case there is a gap and a desire for "better". There is an inbuilt desire in most of us to progress.

Crowdsourcing and online surveys

For many businesses it is simply impossible to have every member of staff attend a workshop. Sam Palmisano's 72-hour "values jam" at IBM in 2003 mentioned earlier was a remarkable but, still today, rare feat. But it doesn't need to be. While face-to-face workshops are hard to beat, crowdsourcing technology has much to offer. Clever online platforms provided by firms such as Synthetron* can be employed to cut across silos that exist inside and outside businesses. Bringing staff, clients, suppliers and partners together helps uncover their concerns and harvest their ideas. Enabling large groups of people from around the world to share their thoughts and intentions with

---

* See www.synthetron.com/homepage-en/

anonymity not only encourages straight talking but tackles some of the issues that come with hierarchical businesses. Crowdsourcing platforms give everyone a voice regardless of rank, role or responsibility. What becomes important is not who said what, but what was said. Using a skilled moderator who is armed with the right questions, a structured crowdsourcing "event" can quickly identify and even rank suggestions and solutions. It is possible to engage up to 1,000 people at one time but a single one hour session involving as few as fifty people can yield rich quantitative and qualitative data.

To understand more about the potential and results of crowdsourcing, James Surowiecki's 2005 book *The Wisdom of Crowds*[5] and Charles Leadbetter's book *We-Think*,[6] published four years later, are both excellent references. But if you don't have the time, in a nutshell their joint message is: a combination of expertise, collective intelligence and the judgement of a crowd are a potent, powerful mix that can deliver remarkable results.

My overall perspective is that seemingly exciting new research models, technology, or widgets are great, but the key to success is collecting the right data, and analysing it well. Gathering masses of data through online surveys and the rest has its place (look at Donald Trump's campaign) as well as measuring everything might satisfy the risk averse. But as Meghann Jones VP Public Affairs of global research company Ipsos pointed out in an interview I had with her, while "big data" might be useful, so far algorithms alone have done a poor job of making automated analytics useful—it still requires humans to look at it, along with other kinds of data, and make sense of what it is telling us.

3 Understanding the social context

Social contribution analysis and social issue identification

In its 2015 sustainability report, the publishing and education multinational Pearson graphically laid out how it identified the 19 social issues of most concern to its stakeholders.[7] Based on this knowledge the company was able to translate these concerns into nine priorities that align directly with three of the UN's Sustainable Development Goals (SDGs).

Through the process Pearson was not only able to understand what the prevalent issues that affect its business performance are, but also how its assets and knowledge can be best directed to tackle them. Pursuing one of four transformative ambitions "to become closer to the people" using its products and services, "The World's Learning Company", as it calls itself, is capitalising on a definition of sustainability that goes beyond the traditional CSR thinking. In doing so, it is beginning a journey and positioning itself for the future around a declared powerful Single Organizing Idea: "to help people make progress in their lives through access to better learning."

What current initiatives fit into what areas?

Charity	Philanthropy	Corporate Social Responsibility	Sustainability	Shared Value
	Charity with direction (Teaching how to fish)	Actions that minimise harm	Actions that assure the resilience of the business	Solving problems that realise a return on investment
Simple acts of kindness (Giving fish)				
Short-term	Long-term	Compliance with standards	Proactively optimizing positive impact across the value chain	Specific focus on increasing profitability
Emotional intervention	Focused on problem solving	Responsible citizenship	Building effective relationships	Achieving competitive advantage
Focused on providing relief	Cause driven	Triple bottom line reporting	Innovation that benefits all stakeholders	Lowering costs
		Building trust	Reducing risk	Driving efficiencies and addressing deficiencies
		Building brand reputation	Core strategy	
		Bolt-on strategy		

Figure 14 Types of social engagement

Assessing and mapping the nature of your current philanthropic and CSR activities is a way to understanding stakeholder concerns. Such analysis will bring clarity to the existing investment being made to society and the nature of it. Understanding the different objectives and types of contribution will help identify the strengths and weaknesses of your overall effort and gauge the impact of philanthropic giving versus CSR "no harm" policies and "win-win" strategies, such as those advocated by the Shared Value Initiative. Ultimately, identifying the issues that affect your business and society will help define your SOI.

Bringing it all together—the hypothesis presentation

Facts, insights and ideas form the backbone of a hypothesis. Combined with intuition these are the key ingredients of a successful hypothesis presentation. Note that I do not say "report". Reports get read (sometimes) and filed (always).

A good hypothesis presentation brings context to life. It delivers evidence, explains "what it all means" and sets out options and finally recommendations that can be practically achieved. The presentation is a culmination of several months' work (how long the research takes depends on the size and complexity of the business). Proper time needs to be set aside for its delivery and the right people need to be in the room. This is not something that can be rushed through—logically set out evidence backed up with hard facts that lay bare the truth of your business will demonstrate a deep understanding of its challenges and its opportunities.

Identifying valuable sources of information, carrying out interviews and gathering research is the easy part. Analysing, understanding and drawing out insights from what's been gathered is somewhat harder. But the really hard part is assembling it in a way that makes sense and leads to informed discussion and sound decisions.

As I mentioned earlier, there are limits to how much research can be done and there are also limits to what can be shared. Balance is absolutely critical in achieving recommendations that have both the authority and the impact necessary to convince the audience that what is being presented is reliable and sufficient.

The hypothesis presentation is not only an opportunity to share insights, conclusions and recommendations, it is an opportunity to gain buy-in and build belief. A lacklustre presentation delivered without conviction will not carry the day. The defining or redefining of a business's Single Organizing Idea, the values that underpin it and the statement that will frame and position it for the future are an important moment. The leadership team needs to be inspired to turn what they're being presented with into a reality. Presentations need to seize the moment, set the tone for the implementation and build momentum.

Steve Jobs delivered an extraordinary hypothesis presentation to his staff and distributors shortly after infamously returning to the business in 1997. Apple was teetering on the verge of bankruptcy when he said: "What people really want to know is who is Apple and what is it that we really stand for?" Dressed in shorts and sandals, he set out what he saw as the single most important thing Apple needed to do to reignite the business—"Getting back to its core values". He explained that while the world changes, the core values of a business should never change and that they shape every part of the business including its marketing (not the other way round). If you watch the video on YouTube[8] you will see that he doesn't mention what the actual values are but he clearly states that their role is to support an aspiration that goes beyond being a technology leader. Apple has a greater purpose, he says. "We believe that people with passion can change the world for the better". Nonchalantly he then introduces a preview of an advertisement that culminates in two words "Think Different". He described it as a marketing campaign but it was something far greater than that; it was a rallying call aimed at galvanizing his staff, and he delivered it with total conviction. It took time, but those two future-defining words—"Think Different"— reignited the values that lay dormant within Apple and set it on a course that made it the most valuable business on the planet. The point is that he didn't return to the company with a made-up set of values, he simply asked that they be rediscovered and defined so that he could articulate and share the purpose of the Apple—and, more importantly, the idea it was single-mindedly organised around—with stakeholders both inside and outside. Personally, I think that was his genius.

8   Phase 2: Defining

Creating a winning strategy

Look up the dictionary definition of a hypothesis and you will see it explained as "a proposed explanation made on the basis of limited evidence that requires further action." The very first action required to turn a hypothesis into a reality is the defining of a strategic framework that spells out exactly what the business stands for and what its purpose is.

As the identifying phase progresses into its final weeks I have found it extremely important to take advantage of scheduled interviews and informal "chats" to share my evolving thoughts with people in the business and in particular with the CEO and the leadership team. Involving people who will ultimately make the strategy real ahead of the hypothesis presentation serves a number of purposes:

- It allows thought processes to be shared
- It provides the opportunity for gaps in knowledge and understanding to be registered and addressed

Mission and vision statements are often forgotten about by most of those in the organization. The elements of the Strategic Framework on the other hand are practical tools that are used every day by everyone in the organisation to shape thinking, make decisions and explain objectives and outcomes.

Single Organizing Idea (SOI)	Values	Positioning statement
An SOI is a simple, memorable call to action. Relevant, compelling and authentic, an SOI succinctly captures the economic and social purpose of your business. It is your guiding star.	Identified through research the values support and underpin the SOI. Each value is a commitment against which actions and ideas can be assessed and monitored. They are carefully selected to help ensure holistic and consistent alignment of your business with the SOI.	The positioning statement frames and explains what the value of the SOI is to your business and to ociety in two or three pithy sentences. It is the elevator pitch.

Figure 15 Strategic framework

- It presents the opportunity to test-run developing theories and gives leadership the opportunity to add their thoughts
- It manages expectation, mitigates surprises and builds a sense of shared endeavour
- Finally, it gives leadership ownership of the strategy before the actual detail is revealed.

The hypothesis and the recommended strategy framework are the result of holding up a mirror to the organization, asking the right questions, working in partnership and finally drawing the right conclusions. It is necessary in defining the content of the strategy framework that what is included really does reflect the truth of the business. Uncovering and confirming truths about the business is the single most important factor in ensuring the framework is built on practical reality and hard facts. There is "word-smithing" involved, but armed with comprehensive insights and ideas, I've found that the three elements of the strategic framework—the SOI, the values and the positioning statement—almost write themselves.

People often ask what comes first when you're writing a strategic framework and the answer is that every programme is different. This is where process stops and creativity takes over. It can take a few hours to write a strategic framework or a few days. How quickly the "aha!" moment comes really does depend on how quickly each part informs the other and the pieces fall into place.

Selecting the values and defining the SOI

Throughout the identifying phase, values, qualities, attributes, commitments, ethics and principles will all be uncovered and discussed. Values mean different things to different people, as we saw in Chapter 3, so it is not unusual at the end of the phase to have identified perhaps ten to fifteen different values or qualities people think are important to the business and themselves. As I said earlier, values matter to people and particularly to Millennials, who want to work for a business that shares theirs. All the values uncovered are likely to be important and they will all mean something positive, but among them will be a few that not only have meaning but also have the greatest potential to help the business advance and achieve its purpose. The objective then is to separate generic values, that simply represent good business practice, from the three or four most relevant values that will support the SOI and ensure consistent, single-minded alignment with it.

It doesn't mean that ethical business values like caring, responsibility and respect are lost; their meaning can be woven into the final selected value descriptions, but the emphasis is on values that establish absolute clarity about what needs to be focused on to ensure the business stays on course and true to its SOI. (As an aside I should say that values like caring, respect, responsibility and integrity are learnt at home and school. People who don't have these values probably shouldn't be working for your business in the first place.)

The values selected are there to set standards, inform culture, drive performance and guide actions. They are the unique qualities the business needs to constantly refer to and act upon if it is to achieve its aim. So in choosing the right values the emphasis needs to be on what qualities will drive the business forward. They will already exist—the objective is to select them and give them the prominence they need. It is critical that they are believed in so they have to be true—not made up.

The earlier story about Jobs and Apple illustrates a point about values. He said Apple needed to "get back to its core values." Some businesses are born with a clear purpose and values but they get lost along the way, as in Apple's case. Anthony Jenkins attempted to reinstate the Quaker values Barclays was founded on. Businesses like The Body Shop, Triodos Bank, Patagonia, Innocent drinks, Ben & Jerry's and Community Clothing are all founded on values and a purpose that were intended to drive a focus on creating profit for the benefit of both business and society. Businesses that have never really defined their purpose or never been consciously values-led undoubtedly face a much greater challenge. But this does not mean that values and purpose don't get uncovered or discovered. It simply means that even greater care and consideration is required to identify the right mix of values and ensure they're firmly grounded in practical reality.

What is clever about Jobs' presentation was it combined hard-edged logic with soft sense appeal. While he talked about "changing the world" at no point did he attempt to frame Apple's purpose in ethical/CSR style packaging. "Think Different" is a single, organization-wide purpose, business philosophy and idea rolled into one that goes beyond the limits of CSR, business ethics and marketing, and addresses the needs of stakeholders.

An SOI and the values that support it are all that is required and, in my experience, all that needs to be remembered to run a business. Which begs the question: "Why is a positioning statement needed?"

Framing the SOI

The positioning statement is the explainer. A business that has an SOI at its core that is of benefit to both shareholders and society needs explaining. The positioning statement captures and frames what the value of the SOI is to your business and society in two or three sentences. It doesn't need to be remembered verbatim by anyone in the business and it doesn't need to be promoted or posted anywhere outside of it, but it still needs to be clear and compelling. The positioning statement summarises the value or benefit of your business to its stakeholders and explains how the functions of the business should be managed and judged. I have found the collective spirit of the values and the SOI to be a good starting point in writing a positioning statement. When you put the values and the SOI all together, what does it say?

What you most definitely should not end up with is the kind of bland mission/vision statements I mentioned in Chapter 6. However, even an organization like Apple is not immune and for a number of years, the standard footer to their corporate communications (press releases, etc) read: "Apple designs Macs, the best personal computers in the world, along with OS X, iLife, iWork and professional software. Apple leads the digital music revolution with its iPods and iTunes online store." It's a long way from Job's single organizing idea to "Think Different" and the statement that framed it: "To make a contribution to the world by making tools for the mind that advance humankind."

9 Phase 3: Aligning

Turning strategy into reality

Someone once told me after the successful presentation of a hypothesis that the room was filled with a "strategic glow." The SOI and the process that generated it might leave you with a sense of satisfaction and in some cases, even relief that you've finally defined and captured your SOI, but unless it is actually implemented and the entire business is aligned with it, it means absolutely nothing.

Peter Drucker once said "Plans are only good intentions unless they immediately degenerate into hard work".[1] In this chapter we look at what that hard work looks like and how the SOI can be implemented and managed.

Stepping off

First of all, it's necessary to establish that the strategic framework has been fully understood. If the SOI is to achieve its full potential then its introduction, implementation and management need to be led from the top of the business. As I alluded to earlier, in my experience CEOs and leadership teams are often fast to respond positively to a well thought through hypothesis that is rooted in hard facts and that they have invested their time and thoughts into. But it is critical that time be taken to allow the strategy to be fully understood and interrogated.

The leadership team must stress test and sanity check the strategic framework. Referring to it and the hypothesis while addressing the questions I have listed in Figure 16 will help them ensure the strategy makes sense and that, most importantly, it is practical. Without getting into detailed tactical considerations it will help them qualify what the risks are over the short, medium and long term and at the same time help them clarify in their own minds what level of commitment they will need to personally apply and demonstrate to make it a success. (No strategy goes without risk and leadership commitment is always required to overcome challenges—more on this in the last chapter).

Criteria	Question	Thoughts
Credible	Is the SOI based on reality/hard facts and evidence?	
Resilient	Will the SOI be sustainable over the long-term regardless of management, technology and market changes?	
Relevant	Does the SOI have value to all types of stakeholders?	
Profitable (win1)	Will the adoption of the SOI make the business more commercially successful?	
Beneficial (win2)	Will the adoption of the SOI benefit people and planet?	
Single	Does the SOI provide a single-minded purpose that will help separate what is important from what is not?	
Organizing	Will the individual functions of the business be able to align and practically contribute to the potential of the SOI?	
Idea	Is the SOI an enriching concept that people will admire and aspire to be a part of?	

Figure 16 Stress-testing the strategy

Armed with their individual assessments, a workshop that brings the leadership team back together, perhaps with key members of your board if you have one, will give them the opportunity to refine the strategic framework (if necessary), and discuss a roadmap that will affect its roll-out over the short to medium term. More importantly it will help frame key objectives, priorities and challenges so that they can be explained to the wider business.

At this point it is important that internal announcements related to the SOI are carefully crafted and delivered. A high degree of transparency is required to ensure the substance behind the SOI is explained and that it will be relevant to and benefit all stakeholders. The nature of these announcements and the way they are delivered will pave the way for the start of the alignment process. Done well, internal communications can build on the open, inclusive nature of the research and analysis phase of the programme to build trust, generate excitement and anticipation; turning the flywheel of momentum that will encourage further contribution. Done badly, the whole project runs the danger of looking like a superficial exercise led by the CEO and the marketing department.

It is crucial to stress in these early communications that, while the SOI will provide the focal point for the business going forward, it will take time for the benefits of it to be fully understood and realised. Potential and evolution not revolution needs to be a key message, especially if your business is not based on a modern flat structure but on traditional hierarchical lines. Inevitably carrying on with the old way of doing things is much easier than stretching and extending oneself to reach new objectives, especially if the point of doing so is not immediately clear. All businesses are different. Culture, morale, resources, commitments, calendars, organizational setup, brand identity/ies, relationships, organizational structure, processes, practices and understanding among many other factors play a role in dictating the pace of change and the evenness of it across the board. While some functions and elements of your business may align themselves quickly with the SOI others may take a considerable amount of time to do so. In 1999 John M.T. Balmer, Professor of Corporate Marketing at Brunel University, published his ACID Test to help explain the "journey" different stakeholders travel along to reach what he described as an ideal "total alignment".[2] I first came across it when I was working for WPP's brand consultancy Enterprise IG and have since adapted it to help explain alignment with an SOI (Figure 16).

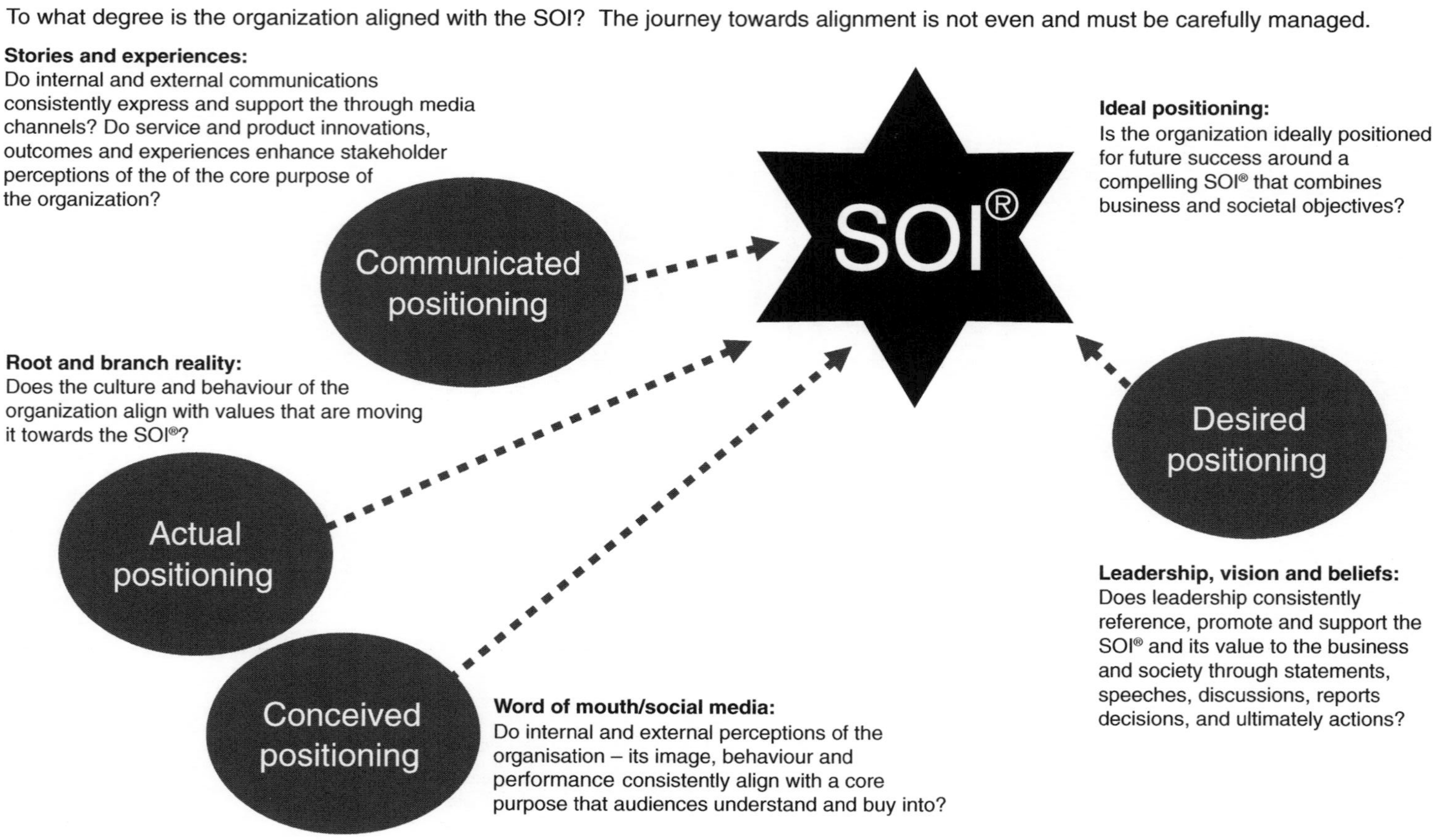

To what degree is the organization aligned with the SOI? The journey towards alignment is not even and must be carefully managed.

Stories and experiences:
Do internal and external communications consistently express and support through media channels? Do service and product innovations, outcomes and experiences enhance stakeholder perceptions of the of the core purpose of the organization?

Ideal positioning:
Is the organization ideally positioned for future success around a compelling SOI® that combines business and societal objectives?

Leadership, vision and beliefs:
Does leadership consistently reference, promote and support the SOI® and its value to the business and society through statements, speeches, discussions, reports decisions, and ultimately actions?

Root and branch reality:
Does the culture and behaviour of the organization align with values that are moving it towards the SOI®?

Word of mouth/social media:
Do internal and external perceptions of the organisation – its image, behaviour and performance consistently align with a core purpose that audiences understand and buy into?

SOI®

Desired positioning

Communicated positioning

Actual positioning

Conceived positioning

Figure 17 Alignment with the SOI

Stepping up

With this picture firmly in mind you shouldn't think about the approach to aligning with an SOI as a purely sequential process of time and effort that is set at one pace across your business. Instead it should be viewed as an ongoing "constant" that relies upon different levels of commitment and action at different times from different parts of your business. It is like moving up a staircase of steps of varying heights along a line of upward progress.

Alignment with an SOI looks simple on paper but its implementation is rarely straightforward and in my experience never complete. The principles of continuous improvement (Kaizen) play a substantial role in affecting change associated with the adoption and embedding of an SOI.

Alignment clearly means change—and with change comes risk. De-risking the process doesn't just demand clear communications and the establishment of trust. It requires that planned actions deliver tangible outcomes that demonstrate the potential of the SOI.

One immediate benefit of an SOI is that it very quickly brings your business together under a single banner. It also brings with it a single issue to solve: How do we carry on the day job and at the same time transition to a business aligned with an SOI that is quite different from where we are today? Applying the skills, expertise and intelligence of the people in your business to the task of achieving that objective will not only unite them around a common cause but at the same time encourage cooperation and

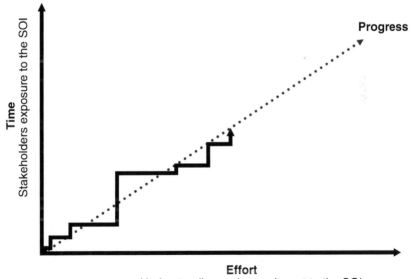

Achieving total alignment with the SOI takes time and effort. The pace of change and the ability to adapt is determined by a host of factors including culture, heritage, leadership, organizational structure, business priorities, market forces, investment and resources.

Figure 18 Time and effort steps

collaboration. But there will be hurdles to jump, including the fact that, up until the point of introducing the SOI, it is highly likely that internal teams and their external partners have, in the absence of such a mechanism, been happily pursuing a course that progresses their individual silo.

Ensuring cooperation gives root to the SOI effectively means giving the separate functions of your business the time, responsibility, resources and tools to adjust and carry out the measures required to achieve alignment with it. Importantly while I describe the contribution each function can make individually, they need to been seen as interdependent entities unifying themselves around the SOI. The desired outcome is, after all, instead of being organized around the separate functions of your business, your functions are pulling together around a Single Organizing Idea.

Aligning communications

Smart internal and external communications should remind, support and underline the value of the SOI in a way that engages stakeholders with it and invites contributions to it.

I have already indicated the level of care that needs to be taken with communications. Care should be the watchword concerning all communications, both internal and external. We have looked at the consequences of brand and reputation in Chapter 5, so there is no need to repeat the points here. Instead I'll simply emphasize that the enormous pride often felt at the launch of an SOI off the back of emotionally moving communications promising change for the better, can quickly turn sour and fizzle out into a cosmetic makeover.

In my experience, advertising and PR agencies, in particular, need to be extremely carefully managed and controlled by communications directors to ensure that passionate but misguided creative brilliance and short-term financial gain do not generate unintentional consequences. Damaged reputation along with eroding trust and loyalty can easily undermine a genuine commitment to changing the core of your business.

The problem with BP's infamous strapline to go "beyond petroleum" was that only some of parts of the business was actually doing so or intended to do so. In his 2015 book *Connect: How Companies Succeed by Radically Engaging Society*, CEO and architect of the vision, Lord John Browne says that what he deeply regrets more than anything was the failure to manage the gap between aspiration and reality.[3] In other words, the rhetoric didn't line up with what was actually happening. The advertising agency involved probably wouldn't have liked the lack of slickness and neat fit with the BP name, but "Going Beyond Petroleum" rather than "Beyond Petroleum" would have been more open, accurate and less incendiary.

A communications plan that includes a risk assessment needs to be developed by communications managers. It should draw on external professionals and representatives from other parts of the business to ensure false expectations are not unintentionally broadcast, and an open and honest picture of your business is projected to stakeholders—those it is hoped—who will ultimately invest, work for and buy products and services from your organization.

The SDG Compass guide has an excellent section dedicated to the topic of reporting and communicating progress against the SDGs which is extremely relevant to the successful embedding of an SOI.[4]

Aligning products and services

Experiences are mainly created by contact with the quality and performance of your products and services. Alignment with an SOI that benefits all stakeholders can help ensure user experiences are positive, consistent and satisfying. To achieve this, your products and services must align or be capable of alignment with the SOI and the values that underpin it.

It goes without saying that the stronger the connection to the SOI, the more likely continuity will reinforce the overall objective of alignment with an SOI. If your business relies upon cash cows targeted at customers in markets that don't or can't align with your SOI then that needs very careful consideration. Carrying out an analysis of your product and service portfolio that includes inputs from key internal and external stakeholders and experts will help identify which products and services fit with the SOI and which don't. Evaluating the outcomes of the analysis will help create a transition strategy to alignment with the SOI that includes goal setting, research and development, implementation, monitoring and feedback. I have mentioned Unilever on a number of occasions throughout this book. Talking to people connected to that business is interesting because you see the effort that is being made to align the portfolio of products and the way it does business with Polman's Sustainable Living Plan, and the challenges that arise during that journey. WWF's 2015 assessment of Unilever, published in April 2016, ranked it as a company "leading the way" on palm oil usage.[5] In November of the same year, Amnesty International slammed Unilever in a damming report. Meghna Abraham, a Senior Investigator at Amnesty International told Jonathan Webb, a *Forbes* magazine contributor, that "Corporate giants like Colgate, Nestlé and Unilever assure consumers that their products use 'sustainable palm oil', but our findings reveal that the palm oil is anything but,".[6]

Aligning systems and processes

How your business gets things done and the way in which you manage quality and efficiency directly impacts the sustainability of your business. As mentioned earlier, Marks and Spencer's Plan A is a leading example of what can be achieved as a result of a thorough review of systems and processes driven by a desire to address supply chain challenges that affect people, planet and profit.

In other sectors, such as agribusiness, there is a very urgent need to address supply chain sustainability. "As our clients face environmental and geopolitical factors that are conspiring to threaten the fundamental pillars of their businesses, they are having to find ways to address what were typically thought of as development challenges and ensure that they can endure into the future," explains Meghann Jones, VP Public Affairs for Ipsos. "Cocoa farming is one of the sectors that we observe to be taking this very seriously. Here you see the conflation of multiple serious development challenges presenting a significant threat to the future of the business—poverty, urbanization, environmental threats, land rights, slavery and child labour, to name a few. Programs like the Mondelēz Cocoa Life program are making a real attempt to address some of these challenges. They have to deliver an ethical product to consumers, and they have to demonstrate to shareholders that they are able to stay in business for the long term."

Establishing and reinforcing best practice beyond the supply chain and into the day-to-day operational and capital decisions through the lens of an SOI will ensure that standards and approaches are consistent at every touch point of your business.

Aligning innovation

Unfortunately I have come across very few businesses that run innovation programmes designed to involve all their staff in the development of fresh ideas. Businesses may have an R&D facility but this is not the same as creating mechanisms that nurture ideas that engage and impact the whole business. When you have an SOI at the core of the business that staff not only understand but helped define, it presents a huge opportunity to change that. A business can immediately widen the scope of possible benefits both to it and society by challenging staff, through a structured programme, to dedicate time and effort to thinking about fresh ideas aligned with the SOI. As well as unlocking and stretching the collective wisdom of the people in your business, such a programme involves and recognizes their efforts. Innovation programmes that create forums within the business, possibly linked to networks outside it, generate energy, garner support and underline the need for continuous improvement in line with the SOI. If you regularly monitor and communicate the progress of innovations that are both in development and delivered, you can maintain momentum and underline that the SOI is part and parcel of the day-to-day life of your business.

Of course many businesses have given people the means to innovate. Toyota empowering its people to stop the production line at any time to suggest improvements is a famous case in point. But probably a better example is Google's approach to ensuring all its people have an innovation role. Its 70-20-10 rule stipulates that 70% of an employee's time should be spent on core duties; 20% on activities that advance the business and 10% on activities that advance the individual. The result is not only a flow of fresh thinking aligned with Google's "universal accessibility" SOI, but a dynamic business culture that thrives and takes pride in its ability to continually move forward and adapt. Creating an innovation programme that benefits both your business and society will stimulate, motivate and make your business more dynamic.

Aligning culture and behaviour

Alignment with a relevant, compelling SOI that delivers tangible and intangible benefits to your staff can help build a positive unified culture that celebrates high performance and shared success.

It is critical that all staff understand and are aligned with the SOI and the values that underpin it. The ideas, customs, beliefs and behaviours of people is the number one determining factor dictating how successful alignment will be. Simply put, without the buy-in and on-going support of staff, none of the other areas of alignment can be attempted. But challenging long-held practices, behaviours and attitudes and aligning them with new thinking is a tough task, as I will consider in the final chapter.

Businesses need to carefully introduce a structured approach that encourages and involves, but doesn't prescribe. The objectives and benefits of workshops and training sessions need to be meaningful to the individual as well as to the business if change is to happen. Workshops, crowdsourcing and feedback mechanisms that allow staff to explore ideas and define objectives will empower them to assess and reach conclusions themselves. When an SOI benefits society, and when staff contributed their ideas to it during the identifying phase, they are usually more than willing to accept the values, standards and new practices that ensure consistency. Delivered in the right way, the introduction of these new dynamics will seem like common sense.

As I have stressed earlier, it takes time; without first understanding and then seeing the positive results of change, some staff will be reluctant to fully commit and participate in it. But in my experience once it begins to happen it's often the most cynical and vocal opponents of change that are the first to fully embrace and, quite often, champion it. Aligning culture and behaviour with an SOI is about winning hearts and minds and that is only ever achieved over time. A successful culture programme makes the SOI the ultimate concern of everyone in the business and helps ensure that every action and behaviour of the business and its people flows from the SOI.

Aligning design

Like the word "brand", "design" is associated with skin-deep superficiality. However, in respect of an SOI, design—particularly visual identity—plays a crucial role in transforming the business. How the SOI is perceived is largely based on how it is seen. A strong visual identity that appeals to the senses delivers impact, builds awareness, amplifies meaning and makes the SOI accessible. External design expertise should be engaged to create guidelines that ensure alignment with the SOI is expressed at every touch point. Clear signposting that makes it easier for audiences to view and understand the benefits of your SOI and, importantly, your single-minded pursuit of it, builds trust.

The same caution should be exercised in choosing your design agency as your advertising or PR agency. I always recommend a "beauty parade" of agencies be carried out that includes the incumbents. These are key partnerships and the task is too important to get wrong. A complete change of talent or shoring up existing talent should be seriously considered.

An SOI takes ambiguity out of the business strategy. The SOI links the internal and external experts working in the different silos of the business through a common objective. Successful alignment unites otherwise competing teams and builds commitment and consensus holistically.

Figure 19 Alignment of business functions

Activating your SOI

It is quite possible that your business is already doing things across its functions that align with the SOI. In other words, your business is not likely to be starting from scratch.

In Chapter 2, I introduced you to Nick Davies and Neighbourly and promised we'd return. Of all the start-ups bringing digital technology to bear on achieving a more sustainable future, few have the ambition and scale of UK based Neighbourly.

To re-cap, Nick had undertaken to build a single digital platform where brand initiatives could co-exist and connect with a marketplace of community projects. Like others, he recognised that no company can tackle the planet's environmental and societal challenges on their own; his solution sought to amplify collective contribution and, in turn, accelerate the sustainable business movement. But if businesses were to unite behind a common platform, that platform would need to deliver a huge and highly automated service proposition—everything from deployment of funding and management of employee volunteering to efficient distribution of product and surplus.

That would be no small undertaking and yet even this wouldn't go far enough. As Nick explains, "even if you successfully unified all corporate giving such that every company saw benefit in joining in, you'd still only be achieving "more CSR". That would be an incredible achievement of course, but actually it would put you on the cusp of something even more exciting— the chance to unlock the true potential of citizens all around the world by turning companies into catalysts."

What does "companies as catalysts" mean? Nick has already proven that consolidating CSR into a single platform quickly attracts thousands of projects and many more users. This core of community activists then shares projects across their social networks which drives exponential user growth, in turn attracting more companies. As these companies successfully align their existing CSR efforts and increase their contribution (for example, starting with food surplus then adding employee volunteering) they increasingly use their own communication channels and then advertising spend to promote what they're doing, driving platform awareness still further. It's at that point that a company is truly ready to graduate from CSR to creating shared value, or CSV.

"As companies become more coordinated with CSR and increasingly comfortable with their SOI, they stop listening out for tactical opportunities and start using Neighbourly to brief society on big bold ideas where their leadership and resources can get people thinking and behaving differently," says Nick. "After all, great brands and their advertising agencies are the masters of inspiration and influence—imagine the impact that could be achieved if companies used their creative brilliance to inspire fans to 'be neighbourly'—to contribute a little of their own time and money and join

Investing in the four steps shown here will help determine your progress towards alignment with the SOI

Step	Action
Step 1	Engage staff and external experts to translate the strategy into specific objectives that can be executed across all the functions of your business.
Step 2	Draw up detailed plans to achieve the objectives by developing initiatives that will support the SOI, setting goals and allocating the necessary resources.
Step 3	Design a balanced scorecard system that will help track progress and the impact of the initiatives and the SOI overall.
Step 4	Communicate and celebrate milestones on the path to achieving the objectives and aligning your business with the SOI.

Figure 20 Steps to progress

in where they live? Those that did would change the world whilst simultaneously earning permission to trade in a future that looks pretty bleak for companies who fail to step up."

Neighbourly already helps companies like Marks & Spencer, The Body Shop, Starbucks, Lidl and Heineken run activation campaigns and connect all forms of corporate giving in the U.K. and is set to grow the movement internationally in the next 12 months. It is a compelling proposition and I'm hopeful it can be the activation tool to complement any company's SOI.

In concluding this chapter, it is important to summarise that alignment with an SOI requires tackling a steep learning curve. The truth is very few people in a business will have experienced such a transition before. Although they may have change management experience it will most likely not be quite like what has been described above. What is critical is that the SOI remains front of mind, and that a holistic view of the business is adopted. As I have witnessed through my own experiences, it is easy for organizations to go off on tangents. The SOI is there to ensure that you stay focused and that the initiatives you decide to pursue through the different functions of your business remain true to it and support it. There will never be a day when you arrive at the end goal, so success is not about crossing a finishing line. Success is about sustaining progress; moving forward and reaching milestones that enhance the value of your business in the eyes of all your stakeholders.

10 What it takes

In his 1991 book *Commitment: The Dynamic of Strategy,* the acclaimed economist, strategist and global commentator Pankaj Ghemawat wrote: "Commitment is the only general explanation for sustained differences in the performance of organizations." He went on to say: "What needs to be emphasized is that the degree of commitment in regard to choices ensures that they can lead to sustained differences rather than merely transient ones."[1]

In other words, when competitors are matched in every other way—in the same markets, with the same objectives, issues, opportunities and, unsurprisingly, often the same strategies—it is the businesses that are totally committed to seeing through the choices they've made that win out at the end of the day. Commitment over a sustained period of time, he argues, is the only real differentiator between one competitor and another.

One of the greatest benefits of an SOI is its ability to focus the mind on what is and is not important. These are the choices the business needs to make in order to survive and develop. The single-minded pursuit of an SOI brings clarity of purpose to your business that, in turn, brings clarity to the choices it needs to make.

Empowering your employees to determine what your business should start, stop and keep doing to align with the SOI across all your business functions is a goal worth striving for. But unless people are engaged and committed to making those choices in the first place, your SOI will quickly become an unrealized ideal that without proof of beneficial outcomes will eventually fizzle out.

No matter how compelling the SOI, no matter how obvious its benefits, without the collective will of your business to embrace and see it through, its full potential will never be realized. Gaining total commitment to the SOI is without doubt the key to success. So what stands in the way of achieving total commitment?

In this final chapter I want to share my first-hand experiences from the past three decades and offer some thoughts around what I believe are the two biggest barriers to gaining total commitment. The obstacles can be summarized as leadership appetite and organizational culture. The antidote that can help deliver total commitment is investing adequately in change.

Leadership appetite

"The SOI is definitely right, but I'm concerned about my senior management team delivering it." This was the message I got from the CEO of a UK tech company shortly after my presentation was over and the "strategic glow" had dimmed. It's a message I've heard many times before and it's mainly about attitude, not ability. For some senior managers the clarity of a single purpose, organized around a compelling idea, is an exciting prospect that can't come soon enough. For others it is an unnecessary step in the dark that, despite the benefits, fills them with understandable trepidation.

The truth is that successful alignment with an SOI doesn't require the kind of leadership skills and approaches that old-fashioned, top-down-minded business managers all too often rely upon. Its implementation doesn't require that the power of decision-making be concentrated in one place at the top of the business. Nor does it require hard-nosed "business is business" platitudes, nor people who play politics, nor those who use jargon to hide behind their titles, or more dubiously, behind their responsibilities.

What successful alignment does require is genuine, flexible leaders who are prepared to put their egos to one side, open their minds, learn, adapt and change their approach if necessary. Alignment with an SOI encourages the development of a modern business approach: one that thrives on the dispersal of power, collaboration, transparency and trust.

The kind of business that most people aspire to be a part of today has leaders who understand their role as proactive facilitators and enablers equipped to convince, inspire and encourage. These are leaders that are dedicated to generating the energy and momentum required to set and reach shared objectives and ultimately a shared purpose. They will draw on their personal values and the values of the business to build dynamic teams and develop internal and external relationships. They can cultivate a business environment that celebrates and recognizes the value of curiosity, constant learning, empathy and improvement.

These are explicit attributes but they are not the unattainable characteristics of a rare breed of gifted "born leaders". Rather, they are the traits of experienced managers who are prepared to set aside personal differences and departmental rivalries to lead by example. The shared sense of purpose that an SOI brings is a big part of the solution to the fast-changing world I described in Part 2 of this book. But without leaders who can communicate and connect people, and ensure everyone shares a common view of what the SOI is and what their role is in achieving it, the opportunity to change for good will be lost.

Leadership is not easy—it can be extraordinarily challenging. Just like commitment, real leadership is a choice that demands individuals to stand up and take it on. How leaders behave, what they do and how they do it sets the tone and influences outcomes.

Sean Riches is a practicing management consultant and visiting lecturer in organizational change at Kings College, London. He has some ideas about leadership. He has been hired worldwide by the likes of Unilever, Oracle and Paramount Films among many others, and I have known him since we put our leadership training wheels on at London University Officer Training Corps in the early 1980s.

Thirty years on I invited Sean to write a short article on leadership for my consultancy's quarterly publication.* Drawing on his well of experience and citing everyone from John Adair and his 'Action Centred Leadership' model, to Professor Paul Hersey's book *The Situational Leader*, Ken Blanchard's *The One Minute Manager* and Daniel Goleman's *Emotional Intelligence*, Sean captured the trends, moments in history and leaders that have shaped our thoughts on leadership since World War One. He ended with management expert Gary Hamel's observation that in a modern business "...talent and ideas will come from all over an organization." Sean concluded that that doesn't mean you don't need leadership to harness all that energy. But he added: "... if you can't do that then the key leadership activity you may want to consider is to get over yourself and get out of the way". I couldn't agree more.

Organizational culture

Organizational culture is another big barrier to the success of an SOI. At this point, and even though we've touched on the subject before, let's just have a clear understanding of what exactly culture is.

For me Edgar Schien, the former professor at MIT Sloan School of Management and recognized leading light in the field for 50 years, comes closest to my own personal understanding of culture. He sees it as a constantly changing phenomena that no one individual can ever totally see or explain.

Schien cleverly uses an iceberg to describe his theory of organizational culture.[2] At the top of the iceberg, visible to everyone, are the "artefacts". These "artefacts" are the tangible and identifiable elements of your business. Logos, advertising, dress codes, physical structures, online and off-line environments, staff behaviour, work policies and practices are among the elements I described as "touch-points" that stakeholders experience in Chapter 8.

One level down, just below the surface, lie "espoused values". These values are taken up and espoused by leadership to help explain and promote

---

*   Glance is Neil Gaught & Associates' quarterly publication written by its Associates, Partners and invited Experts. www.neilgaught.com/glance.html

the objectives of a business. These then should be the "ideal values" your business needs to align itself with to succeed in achieving its purpose and alignment with the SOI.

In the murky depths below these espoused values lurks what Schien describes as "assumptions". Assumptions are the unwritten "actual values" of your business. Undefined, and in mature businesses possibly unchallenged for decades, these assumptions will have given rise to deep-seated beliefs, traditions and rituals that have shaped the history of your business and its story. Influenced by forces inside and outside your business these assumptions are the barometers of attitude against which potential changes and challenges to culture are unconsciously measured and assessed.

Glimpsed through the potentially distorted lens of company vetting websites such as Glassdoor, these invisible assumptions are often used to explain what the real culture of the business is and "how things really get done."

This vivid description fits exactly with my first-hand experiences as a consultant who has had the benefit of engaging with staff in workshops designed to allow them to describe the gap between ideal espoused values and actual assumed values. From Wall Street banks that spend small fortunes on human capital development, to global professional service firms that employ thousands of people around the world, to centuries old faith-based organizations, to cutting-edge tech businesses that employ less than 30 people—every organization I have ever worked with has mirrored Schien's description. All businesses differ but in this aspect they don't. And it doesn't matter how noble the purpose, nor how clear the values—think of the Catholic Principles, or the intelligence of the workforce—think again of Andersen Consulting and "the smartest guys in the room". In every single case there is always, always a gap between the espoused values that serve to help the organization achieve its goals and move forward, and the unwritten assumptions/values that serve to achieve other purposes. Identifying the individual values from Schien's third level that will drive your business forward, and separating them from those that don't, is the most important objective of the identifying phase. Values cannot be adopted, borrowed or made up—they need to come from within the heart of the business.

The difference between a highly committed culture, where staff believe in and draw satisfaction from being included, engaged and enabled around a single idea they care about, and a culture that pays lip service to values and purpose is one measure of the challenge you face.

The size of the gap and the amount of time it has gone unchecked will give a very rough guide as to how long it may take to achieve alignment with an SOI. And let's face it, the daily reality of many businesses is that interdepartmental rivalries have been allowed to flourish alongside personal ambition, status squabbles, disaffection, uneven fairness, broken promises and uncertainty. There is often passive aggressiveness caused by friction between those who just want to do their jobs, those who have ambitions elsewhere and those who seek "a higher purpose". Add to this the understanding that despite the dysfunction this brings it is, sadly, what people expect and have perhaps become accustomed to.

Not to trivialise it in any way, I can best describe it as wanting someone to give up smoking. Given time, effort, encouragement and a great deal of patience, many will accept the positive outcomes of embracing a new path. But there will always be a hard core that, despite all the evidence, will insist on exercising their personal choice regardless of its impact on them or those around them. That reality, together with the fact that they alone can commit to giving up, needs to be given the utmost respect. At the end it all comes down to commitment.

Investing in change

Having said that, in this fast-paced and increasingly competitive world, it is a nonsense to think we have the time or luxury of letting culture become an insurmountable obstacle. Leaders must step up to the mark and new ideas must be encouraged, and perhaps even enforced.

Beyond the initial investment needed to announce and create excitement around the launch and possibilities of an SOI, on-going investment will be required to sustain its success. It will require a raft of new and, if framed appropriately, exciting measures. The SOI will provide a useful vehicle through which new incentive schemes, improved management frameworks, enhanced internal communications and engagement programmes can be introduced.

Investments will need to be made in training and in the introduction of reward schemes that go beyond the recognition of money-making achievements. They will typically acknowledge ideas that increase productivity, and that encourage actions and behaviours that promote higher levels of performance, enhance culture internally and, of course, positively impact on society externally.

Resources must be allocated to cultivate a climate of change—perhaps even a climate of perpetual change. To get a sense of what is required, I asked Michael Milligan, the CEO of ABET (the world's largest and oldest accreditor of higher education programs in applied science, computing, engineering and engineering technology), to summarise what the successful adoption of an SOI requires. "A great deal of patience, some quiet determination and, of course, an SOI based on a fundamental truth," was his response. He's right. Most corporate executives wrongly assume that associations such as ABET don't have the kind of pressures that come with the need to constantly "delight customers" but in actual fact they do. As Mary Byers, a senior level association executive turned consultant, points out in her book *Road to Relevance*, associations, just like any other organization, face multiple challenges that threaten their very existence.[3] While others have allowed the tides of change to wash away their reason for

The duty of engineers is first and foremost to the public's health and welfare as reflected in ABET's SOI. This societal driven core purpose is different from other professions. For instance doctors' and nurses' duty is to their patients. Accountants', lawyers' and bankers' duty is to their clients.

SOI®	Values	Positioning statement
Assuring Confidence	**Authentic** Our international status as a leading world authority is underpinned by our unique heritage and the longevity of our relationships. By balancing objectivity and sensitivity, we instill trust and realize shared goals and mutual success. **Business-Like** We are defined by our professional approach. Our shared dedication and total commitment to thorough planning and preparation ensure that we deliver world-class results and satisfying experiences. **Expert** Our expertise is based on our knowledge and understanding. by continually challenging ourselves to learn more about the changing needs of academe, industry and the world as a whole, we keep our finger on the pulse and our solutions relevant, fresh and compelling. **Targeted** We set our own targets high. By being single-mindedly focused on constantly achieving new levels of excellence, we deliver results and reassurance for all. By continually measuring and monitoring our performance, we access our progress and practice what we preach.	We champion excellence worldwide. Our approach, the standards we set, and the quality we guarantee inspire confidence in those who aim to build a better world – one that is safer, more efficient, comfortable and sustainable.

Figure 21 ABET's strategic framework

being, ABET's own inclination was to take on these challenges and determine its own future. In doing so, it has won the admiration of many of its peers and at the same time underlined its relevance and value as a force for good in a world that increasingly needs certainty.

It has some way to go and, as I said earlier, there isn't a finishing line to cross, but since the launch of its SOI in April 2015, ABET has increased its efficiencies, enhanced its reputation and opened up brand new opportunities by:

1 redefining its terms of engagement with its employees
2 piloting an innovation program linked to its SOI
3 introducing a programme that supports existing and new societal staff initiatives with the SOI
4 creating a state-of-the-art learning centre at its Baltimore headquarters
5 setting its strategic growth objectives for the next five years aligned with its SOI
6 leveraging the SOI to reduce the size and efficiency of its board
7 putting its purpose and the SDGs at the centre of its annual flagship conference
8 embedding the SOI into all communications, simultaneously stimulating alignment internally and value creation externally
9 employing the values and SOI to enhance the training delivered to the 2,500 experts who carry out accreditation visits around the world on its behalf
10 measuring its progress by carrying out its first internal impact survey
11 winning awards and recognition for its endeavors.

These are tangible achievements but, best of all, ABET's actions have inspired the sharing of positive stories. At an international development conference I attended in Brussels in early 2016, the head of one of the largest recruitment companies in the sector told me how he was turning away graduates holding degrees in international development and advising them to go back to school and study civil engineering if they wanted to make a difference in the world. I was able to tell him about an organization that was all about encouraging just that.

Conclusion

Having spent the last few chapters telling you how hard an SOI is to implement, I'm going to end by showing you how important it is that you try.

Debswana is a mining company that is jointly owned by the Botswana government and De Beers, the diamond company. In early 2001 while at WPP's brand consultancy Enterprise IG, I was part of a leadership team tasked with helping Debswana implement a brand strategy that was designed to reassure its local and global stakeholders in the wake of the conflict diamond crisis. It proved to be an extraordinary learning experience that sparked a lightbulb moment in me and set me on the course I have pursued ever since.

Like Cadbury, Debswana had set out to make a difference from the start. A difference that was later summed up in one phrase: "Mining the resource, enriching the nation". This simple, single idea at once captured the profit and social objective of the company and its core purpose. Organizing itself and everything it does around this idea has been central to Debswana making an extraordinary contribution not only to its own success, but also to that of an entire country.

To see the full story, go to De Beers' 2014 report: *Turning Finite Resources into Enduring Opportunity*.[4] Here, I'm just giving you the headlines. In 1969, when the Debswana partnership was set up, Botswana was a truly poor nation. With a population of some 600,000 people, there were 40 university graduates in the whole country, and one doctor for every 47,000 people. The average annual income per capita was the equivalent of US$84.

Debswana set out to change all that by using its core business activities to "mine the resource and enrich the nation". It simultaneously invested in infrastructure and in people. It made a point of sourcing wherever possible from local enterprises and it has tried over the last, nearly 50 years now, to extend its operations as far along the value chain as possible. It demonstrates how a commercial operation can work with a whole society for mutual benefit.

Expenditure on mines kick-started other sectors such as construction, financial services and transport. To maximize exposure to the diamond value chain, a diamond valuing company was set up in Botswana in 1971. Then the largest and most sophisticated rough diamond sorting and valuing facility in the world was established. Finally, in 2013 De Beers relocated its international sales function to Gaborone from London. All in support of the philosophy which the SOI enshrines.

It's not all perfect and there are still challenges to be met. Nevertheless, Debswana is genuinely important to Botswana. Diamonds make up 80% of the country's exports and employ one Batswana in every 20. In 2014, for example, Debswana generated total revenue of US$6.9 billion. US$0.3 billion of this was paid in wages to employees—of whom 96% are local people. US$0.6 billion was paid for goods and services to suppliers in Botswana and overseas. US$2.2 billion was paid to the Botswana government through taxes, royalties and dividends. This annual injection enables a huge lift in government spending and Batswana wellbeing.

Fifteen years after my work with Debswana in one of those strange twists of fate, I met Ryan Short—the author of the De Beers report mentioned above—at the Shared Value Initiative Affiliate workshop in Boston. We shared our Debswana stories and he told me more about the independent analysis carried out by the company he works for, South African economic consulting firm Genesis Analytics. Today the people of Botswana have access to free public healthcare and free primary and secondary education. The country's transport, energy and water infrastructures have been developed. There is now one doctor for every 3,300 people and Botswana produced 10,668 graduates in 2014. It is no longer a poor country. GDP per capita is US$7,123 making Botswana an upper-middle income economy, and Debswana continues to be admired from near and far.

I believe the ability of any organization to adapt and change depends ultimately on people's acceptance of the need for change. My worry is that, despite wide acceptance that climate change is real and inequality is increasing, the average citizen is too consumed by the travails of daily life and overwhelmed by our perpetual 24/7 news stream to fully understand the sense of urgency needed if we are to avert monumental changes to our very existence. Neighbourly's "companies as catalysts" thinking is absolutely spot-on but if we are to light the fuse in the first instance and achieve the SDGs, businesses need to make it their priority not to just create a rally call but to establish an imperative. That the commitment to identifying a few simple words captured in a Single Organizing Idea can create that spark is hard to argue against. It is not easy but it's totally worthwhile, totally meaningful and it will make a difference, as I hope will this book.

Sources and inspirations

While not every one of the sources included here is directly referenced in the book (see notes), they have all made a contribution. I have found the books, articles, videos and websites very useful in writing this book. Looking back I can safely say that I have spent most of my time reading rather than writing during this project.

Balmer, J. (2006). *The Nature and Management of Ethical Corporate Identity: Discussion Paper on Corporate Identity, Corporate Social Responsibility and Ethics.* The Braybrooke Press Ltd.

Balmer, J.M.T. & Soenen, G.M. (1999). The Acid Test of Corporate Identity Management™. *Journal of Marketing Management* 15(1-3) pp.69-92. Retreived from www.tandfonline.com/doi/abs/10.1362/026725799784870441

Browne, J. (2011). *Beyond Business.* Phoenix: Orion Books.

Browne, J. (2015). *Connect: How Companies Succeed by Radically Engaging with Society.* Penguin Random House.

Business & Sustainable Development Commission. (2017). *Better Business Better World.* Retrieved from http://report.businesscommission.org/uploads/BetterBiz-BetterWorld_170215_012417.pdf

Branson, R. (2013). *Screw Business as Usual.* Virgin Books.

The B Team & Virgin Unite. (2015). *New Ways of Working.* Retrieved from www.tvwleadershipacademy.nhs.uk/sites/default/files/5.%20New%20Ways%20of%20Working%20(B%20Team%20%26%20Virgin%20Unite%202015)_0.pdf

Byers, M., Coerver, H. (2013) *Road to Relevance.* ASAE Association Management Press.

Collins, J. (2001). *Good to Great.* Random House Business.

Davies, N. (2007, 16 June). The inconvenient truth about the carbon offset industry. *The Guardian.* Retrieved from www.theguardian.com/environment/2007/jun/16/climatechange.climatechange

De Beers (2014). *Turning Finite Resources into Enduring Opportunity.* De Beers, 2014.

Drucker, P. (2007). *Essential Drucker: Classic Drucker Collection.* Routledge.

Eccles, R., Newquist, S., & Schatz, R. (2007). *Reputation and its Risks.* Harvard Business Review.

Edelman (2016). *Edelman Trust Barometer Global Survey.* Retrieved from www. edelman.com/insights/intellectual-property/2016-edelman-trust-barometer/

Edelman. (2017). *Edelman Trust Barometer: Annual Global Study.* Retrieved from www.edelman.com/trust2017/

Elkington, J., & Hailes, J. (1988). *The Green Consumer Guide: From Shampoo to Champagne, How to Buy Goods That Don't Cost the Earth.* Gollancz.

Ericsson. (2016). *Technology for Good: Ericsson Sustainability and Corporate Responsibility Report 2016.* Retrieved from www.ericsson.com/assets/local/about-ericsson/sustainability-and-corporate-responsibility/documents/2016-corporate-responsibility-and-sustainability-report.pdf

Evans, J (2105, 23 November). Vauxhall Zafira fires: is DVSA car safety regulator fit for purpose? *The Sunday Times: Driving.* Retrieved from www.driving.co.uk/news/vauxhall-zafira-fires-is-dvsa-the-car-safety-regulator-fit-for-purpose/

Freedman, L. (2013). *Strategy, A History.* Oxford University Press.

Makower, J. & the Editors of Greenbiz.com. (2017). *The Tenth Annual State of Green Business 2017.* Retrieved from www.greenbiz.com/report/state-green-business-2017

Gallup. (2013). *State of the Global Workplace Report.* Retrieved from www.gallup.com/services/178517/state-global-workplace.aspx

Gladwell, M. (2000). *Tipping Point: How Little Things can make a Big Difference.* Abacus.

Gino, F. (2013). *Sidetracked: Why our Decisions get Derailed, and how we can stick to the Plan.* Harvard Business Review Press.

Gnärig, B. (2015). *The Hedgehog and the Beetle: Disruption and Innovation in the Civil Society Sector.* International Civil Society Centre.

GRI, The UN Global Compact, & The World Business Council for Sustainable Development (WBCSD). (2016). *SDG Compass, The Guide for Business Action on the SDGs.* Retrieved from http://sdgcompass.org/wp-content/uploads/2015/12/019104_SDG_Compass_Guide_2015.pdf

Grafton, L. (2011). *The Shift: The Future of Work is Already Here.* William Collins.

Grafton, L. (2014). *The Key: How Corporations Succeed by Solving the World's Toughest Problem.* McGraw Hill Education.

Ghemawat, P. (1991). *Commitment: The Dynamic of Strategy.* Macmillan.

Goleman, D. (1996). *Emotional Intelligence: Why it can Matter More Than IQ.* Bloomsbury.

Gosden, R. (1995). Greening all the way to the bank. *Arena*, 16, 35-37.

Gore, A. (2014). *The Future.* WH Allen.

Hamel, G. (2012). *What Matters Now. How to Win in a World of Relentless Change, Ferocious Competition, and Unstoppable Innovation.* Jossy-Bass.

Harari, Y.N. (2015). *Sapiens: A Brief History of Humankind.* Vintage.

Hartmann, P, Apaolaza Ibáñez V, Forcada Sainz J, (2005) "Green branding effects on attitude: functional versus emotional positioning strategies", *Marketing Intelligence & Planning*, Vol. 23 Issue: 1, pp.9-29, doi: 10.1108/02634500510577447

Handy, C. (2015).*The Second Curve: Thoughts on Reinventing Society.* Penguin Random House.

Hersey, P. (1984) *The Situational Leader.* Warner Books.

Hodgkinson, G., & Starbuck, W. (2012). *The Oxford Handbook of Organizational Decision Making.* Oxford University Press.

Huffington Post (2009, 24 August). 'United Breaks Guitars': Did It Really Cost The Airline $180 Million?. *The Huffington Post.* Retrieved from www.huffingtonpost.com/2009/07/24/united-breaks-guitars-did_n_244357.html

Ipsos Global Reputation Centre (2015). *The Reputation Council, Latest Findings from the Tenth Sitting.* Retrieved from www.ipsos.com/sites/default/files/Ipsos_Reputation_Council_2015_Report.pdf

Ipsos Global Reputation Centre. (2016). *The Reputation Council, Latest Findings from the Eleventh Sitting.* Retrieved from www.ipsos.com/sites/default/files/2016-11/The-reputation-council-2016_0.pdf

Institute for the Future. (2007). *The Future of Work. The Intersection of Work and Technology.* Retrieved from www.iftf.org/uploads/media/FOW_map_screen.pdf

Issacson, W. (2015). *Steve Jobs: The Exclusive Biography.* Abacus.

Khanna, P. (2016). *Connectography: Mapping the Future of Global Civilization.* Random House Trade.

Klein, N. (1999). *No Logo.* Harper Collins.

Klein, N. (2015). *This Changes Everything.* Penguin Random House.

Leadbeater, C. (2009). *We-Think: Mass Innovation, not Mass Production.* Profile Books.

Mayer, C. (2013). *Firm Commitment: Why the Corporation is Failing us and how to Restore Trust in it.* Oxford University Press.

Mulgan, G. (2013). *The Locust and the Bee: Predators and Creators in Capitalism's Future.* Princeton University Press.

Murray, K. (2013).*The Language of Leaders: How Top CEOs Communicate to Inspire, Influence and Achieve Results.* Kogan Press.

Nielsen. (2015).Consumer-goods' Brands that Demonstrate Commitment to Sustainability Outperform those that don't [Press Release]. Retrieved from www.nielsen.com/ug/en/press-room/2015/consumer-goods-brands-that-demonstrate-commitment-to-sustainability-outperform.html

Nooyi, I. (2011). *Performance with Purpose.* YouTube Video. Retrieved from www.youtube.com/watch?v=BDTVdX-enr4

OECD/UNDP. (2016). *Making Development Co-operation More Effective: 2016 Progress Report.* OECD Publishing. Retrieved from www.keepeek.com/Digital-Asset-Management/oecd/development/making-development-co-operation-more-effective_9789264266261-en#.WLlnXhicZE4#page1

Olins, W. (2004). *On Brand.* Thames & Hudson.

Olins, W. (2014). *Brand New. The Shape of Brands to Come.* Thames & Hudson.

Oxfam. (2016). *An Economy for the 1%: How Privilege and Power in the Economy Drive Extreme Inequality and how this can be stopped.* Retrieved from www.oxfam.org/sites/www.oxfam.   org/files/file_attachments/bp210-economy-one-percent-tax havens-180116-en_0.pdf

Pearson (2015). *Transforming our impact: Pearson sustainability report, 2015.* Retrieved from www.pearson.com/content/dam/one-dot-com/one-dot-com/global/Files/sustainability/2015-report/full-2015-report.pdf

Poushter, J. (2015). *Measuring the 'Good' Life Around the World.* Pew Research Centre. Retrieved from www.pewresearch.org/fact-tank/2015/10/29/measuring-the-good-life-around-the-world/

PwC. (2015). *Putting Purpose to Work: A Study of Purpose in the Workplace.* Retrieved from www.pwc.com/us/en/about-us/corporate-responsibility/assets/pwc-putting-purpose-to-work-purpose-survey-report.pdf

Peters, S. (2012). *The Chimp Paradox, The Mind Management Programme for Confidence, Success and Happiness*. Vermillion.

Porter, M., & Kramer, M. (2011).*Creating Shared Value: How to Reinvent Capitalism and Unleash a Wave of Innovation and Growth*. Harvard Business Review.

Roddick, A. (2000). *Business as Unusual, My Entrepreneurial Journey, Profits with Principles*. Harper Collins.

Schien, E. (2010). *Organizational Culture and Leadership – 4th Edition*. Jossey-Bass.

Smiley, A. (2015). *Fast Company 'What Millennial Employees Really Want'*. Retrieved from www.fastcompany.com/3046989/what-millennial-employees-really-want

Steiber, A. (2013).*The Google Model: Managing Continuous Innovation in a Rapidly Changing World*. Springer Cham Heidelberg.

Surowiecki, J. (2005). *The Wisdom of Crowds: Why the Many Are Smarter Than the Few*. Abacus.

Unilever. (2015). Unilever Sees Sustainability Supporting Growth [Press Release]. Retrieved from www.unilever.co.uk/news/press-releases/2015/unilever-sees-sustainability-supporting-growth.html

Unilever. (2015). *Lifebuoy Way of Life Towards Universal Handwashing with Soap: Social Mission Report – 2015*. Retrieved from www.unilever.com/Images/lifebuoy-way-of-life-2015_tcm244-418692_en.pdf

UN Global Compact. www.unglobalcompact.org/about

United Nations (UN). (2015). *Sustainable Development Goals*. Retrieved from www.un.org/sustainabledevelopment/sustainable-development-goals/

United Nations (UN). (2015). *The Millennium Development Goals Report 2015*. Retrieved from www.un.org/ millenniumgoals/2015_MDG_Report/pdf/MDG percent202015 percent20rev percent20(July percent201).pdf

de Wit, M., Wade M., & Schouten, E. (2006) Hardwiring and softwiring corporate responsibility: A vital combination. *Corporate Governance, 6*(4), 491-505.

Wade, M. (2006). A commitment to sustainable development – the long journey begins. In M.J. Epstein, & K.O. Hanson (eds.). *The Accountable Corporation. Volume 3 Corporate Social Responsibility* (pp. 133-46). New York, NY: Praeger.

Wade, M. (2006). Developing leaders for sustainable business. In T. Maak, & N.M. Pless (eds). *Responsible Leadership* (pp. 227-44). London: Routledge.

Webb, J. (2016, 30 November). Amnesty International Slams Colgate, Nestlé and Unilever For Palm Oil Supply Chain Abuses. *Forbes*. Retrieved from www.forbes.com/sites/jwebb/2016/11/30/amnesty-international-slams-colgate-nestle-and-unilever-for-palm-oil-supply-chain-abuses/#1470fb514ea3

Wired Magazine.

The World Business Council for Sustainable Development (WBCSD). www.wbcsd.org

World Wildlife Fund (2016). Palmoil buyers scorecard 2016. Retrieved from http://palmoilscorecard.panda.org/check-the-scores/manufacturers/unilever

Acknowledgments

First and foremost I am eternally grateful for the support, encouragement and love of my wife and best friend Jo. This book would simply not have been possible without the unconditional counsel she gave while reading and listening to successive drafts of every chapter. I also wish to thank my three sons, Harry, Louis and Dillon, for their support and the patience they have shown when the long hours spent on this book have spilled into time that could have been spent with them.

I am especially grateful for the invaluable editing expertise and patience of my friend Wilma Tulloch who at the initial stages of the project brought my muddled thoughts together into some sense of order. Without her clear thinking, encouragement and sense of humour this book would still be a 'singularly disorganised idea.' In addition I also want to thank Matt Whyman for his writing skills and professionalism that helped bring to life the story at the beginning of this book.

I am indebted to the group of expert reviewers who took the time to read drafts of the manuscript. Their assistance in suggesting additional material, correcting mistakes and adding insights vastly improved my understanding, made sense of the points I wanted to make and greatly enriched the final result. Thanks to: David Humphries, Geoff Hunt, Zahid Torres-Rahman, Pattrick Smellie, Avril Macdonald, Mike Barry, Charles Arthur, Nick Davies, Professor David Grayson, and Laurence Evans. I would also like to thank Charles Handy for his time and words of wisdom. Amongst these experts I particularly wish to acknowledge the contribution of my friend and mentor Dr. Mark Wade. Our long discussions not only helped me develop the thinking behind this book but have indeed helped shape my development as a consultant and advisor over the past seven years.

I must make special mention of my many New Zealand friends and colleagues. Their professionalism, independence, easygoing attitude and 'can-do' spirit continues to be a huge inspiration to me. I thank them not only for their friendship and overwhelming support but also for affording me the opportunity to contribute to the country through my minor role as an advisor to New Zealand Trade & Enterprise.

Additionally I need to acknowledge the anonymous contribution the leaders and senior executives of some of the world's largest and most famous companies have made to this book. My role as a consultant has given me unique access to these hugely influential individuals and the opportunity to quiz them on the topics contained in this book. At the same time I also wish to thank the hundreds of employees who work in the for-profit and not-for-profit sectors who I have had the pleasure to meet and discuss the future with through workshops and interviews. The diversity of their backgrounds, beliefs and humanity has had an enormous influence on my world view.

I also want to thank my clients and associates not only for their contributions, support and encouragement but also for their patience and willingness to adjust scheduled calls and meetings so I could work on this book. Among those people are Danielle Duran Baron, Catherine Shovlin, Lucy Clayton, Christina Washburn, Cristian Jurma, Ziad Halaby, Lisa Kingston, Anna Schowengerdt, Lincoln Falconer, Merle Wangerin, Bill Chatwin, Sarah Dorey, Michelle Bouhdoud, David Rutherford, Joanna Collinge, Grant Macdonald, Jonas Christoffersen, Eva Grambye, Judith Cohen, Vivian John-Langba, Nancy McConnell, Aziz Padamsey, Dalia Ouaidat, Louise Kjaer, Lucie Bourgeois, Stine Hattestad Bratsberg, Jan Levy and Paul Linwood and his team.

I need to make special mention of the contribution of Dr. Andrew Moran, Associate Professor of International Relations at London Metropolitan University and his group of students who, as promised, I name individually here: Jarra Fatah (Afghanistan), Sovanvattey Chan (Cambodia), Barrington Roy Schiller (UK), Anamaria Grundill (Romania), Anna Tesarczyk (Germany), Nwokedi Nweke (Nigeria), David Yamalimbu (Democratic Republic of Congo), Matthew Graf (USA), Ivandra Tlanvel (Angola), Beverly Henry-Browne (Trinidad), Derren Teesdale (UK), Rachel Jerome-Graham (Grenada), Patricia Bongo (Democratic Republic of Congo), Johanna Lundgren (Sweden), Mustafa Mohamed Hagi (Ethiopia), Matias Hakala (Finland), Fiona Marschollek (Germany), Anastasia Fouareva (Russia), Amundala Mulolwa (Democratic Republic of Congo), Noer Dayaaldelu (Iraq), Priit Saks (Estonia), Jonathan Martin Brennan (Spain), Parashevas Ntasios (Greece), Alex Kesic (USA), Anne Taylor (Zambia), Sidmira Mondinga (Sao Tome and Principe), Jeanette Damas (Angola), Donela Miguel (Mozambique), Amin Sharif (Somalia).

It is my good fortune to have been Jamie Keenan's friend since we were both design undergraduates at the London College of Printing in the 1980s. He read the manuscript and despite his busy schedule agreed to design the cover for this book without hesitation. The result is beyond what I imagined. Thank you.

In the latter stages of the project Jonathan Glennie took up the challenge of writing the forward and I am grateful to him for his expertise, experience and insights. In addition I am also grateful for the support of his American-based Ipsos colleague Meghann Jones. Jesus really is a Rochdale Girl and

Meghann's knowledge and down to earth pragmatism helped put into context the invaluable research she provided.

Finally special thanks needs to go to my assistant Jackie Tearne who has helped coordinate the team that produced this book. Within that team are the wonderful people at Greenleaf Publishing—Rebecca Marsh, Victoria Halliday, Neil Walsh, John Peters—the team at Routledge and at the UK's leading social change PR agency Forster—Peter Gilheany, Amanda Powell-Smith and Jilly Forster. Thank you all!

Notes

Part 1

Introduction

1 Business & Sustainable Development Commission. (BSDC) (2017). *Better Business Better World*. Retrieved from http://report.businesscommission.org/uploads/BetterBiz-BetterWorld_170215_012417.pdf
2 GRI, The UN Global Compact, & The World Business Council for Sustainable Development (WBCSD). (2016). *SDG Compass, The Guide for Business Action on the SDGs*. Retrieved from http://sdgcompass.org/wp-content/uploads/2015/12/019104_SDG_Compass_Guide_2015.pdf

Part 2

Introduction

1 Khanna, P. (2016). *Connectography: Mapping the Future of Global Civilization*. Random House Trade.

Chapter 1

1 Oxfam. (2016). *An Economy for the 1%: How Privilege and Power in the Economy Drive Extreme Inequality and how this can be stopped*. Retrieved fromwww.oxfam.org/sites/www.oxfam.   org/files/file_attachments/bp210-economy-one-percent-tax havens-180116-en_0.pdf
2 Mayer, C. (2013). *Firm Commitment: Why the Corporation is Failing us and how to Restore Trust in it*. Oxford University Press.
3 Thinkers50. Retrieved from http://thinkers50.com
4 Porter, M., & Kramer, M. (2011).*Creating Shared Value: How to Reinvent Capitalism and Unleash a Wave of Innovation and Growth*. Harvard Business Review.
5 United Nations (UN). (2015). *Sustainable Development Goals*. Retrieved from www.un.org/sustainabledevelopment/sustainable-development-goals/
6 2 Degrees network. Retrieved from www.2degreesnetwork.com/groups/2degrees-community/resources/shared-value-creates-opportunities-business-but-how-do-you-get-there-just-ask-diane-eshleman/
7 Ban Ki-moon's words were read out out by Georg Kell, Executive Director of the UN Global Compact in a special address read at the Sedex Global

Responsible Sourcing Conference 2015. Retrieved from www.youtube.com/watch?v=E5ZsseOWu-4&list=PLrXfQVsW-j_eqawDZ_pGV9Jn2WrBwA5r1

8   Khanna, P. (2016). *Connectography: Mapping the Future of Global Civilization.* Random House Trade.

9   Retrieved from http://fortune.com/2015/08/20/change-the-world-business-model/

10   Financial Times. (2015, 9 February). Paul Polman's socially responsible Unilever falls short on growth. Retrieved from www.ft.com/content/7c79452e-ae5c-11e4-8188-00144feab7de

11   Haid, P. (2015, 28 May). 4 Companies leading the next wave of profit with purpose. *Fast Company.* Retrieved from www.fastcompany.com/3046684/4-companies-leading-the-next-wave-of-profit-with-purpose

Chapter 2

1   Davies, N. (2007, 16 June). The inconvenient truth about the carbon offset industry. *The Guardian.* Retrieved from www.theguardian.com/environment/2007/jun/16/climatechange.climatechange

2   International Organization for Standardization. (2010) *ISO 26000 - Social responsibility.* Retrieved from www.iso.org/iso-26000-social-responsibility.html

3   Wade, M. (2006). A commitment to sustainable development – the long journey begins. In M.J. Epstein, & K.O. Hanson (eds.). *The Accountable Corporation. Volume 3 Corporate Social Responsibility* (pp. 133-46). New York, NY: Praeger.

4   Wade, M. (2006). Developing leaders for sustainable business. In T. Maak, & N.M. Pless (eds). *Responsible Leadership* (pp. 227-44). London: Routledge.

5   de Wit, M., Wade M., & Schouten, E. (2006) Hardwiring and softwiring corporate responsibility: A vital combination. *Corporate Governance,* 6(4), 491-505.

6   Huffington Post (2016, 9 May). Doing well by doing good. *The Huffington Post.* Retrieved from www.huffingtonpost.com/alexandre-mars/doing-well-by-doing-good-_1_b_9860128.html

7   Makower, J. & the Editors of Greenbiz.com. (2017). *The Tenth Annual State of Green Business 2017.* Retrieved from www.greenbiz.com/report/state-green-business-2017

8   Barclays debate: Is CSR dead? Retrieved from www.youtube.com/watch?v=Kdu01FhtngU

9   Elkington, J., & Hailes, J. (1988). *The Green Consumer Guide: From Shampoo to Champagne, How to Buy Goods That Don't Cost the Earth.* Gollancz.

10   Gosden, R. (1995). Greening all the way to the bank. *Arena,* 16, 35-37.

11   Tourism New Zealand. *What we do: Campaigns and activity.* Retrieved from www.tourismnewzealand.com/about/what-we-do/campaign-and-activity/

12   Hartmann, P. (2005). Green branding effects on attitude: functional versus emotional positioning strategies. *Marketing Intelligence and Planning,* 23(1).

Chapter 3

1   *The Economist* (2007, 23 August). Snarling all the way to the bank. Retrieved from www.economist.com/node/9681074

2   *The Telegraph* (2013, 19 September). Ryanair 'worst' brand for customer service. Retrieved from www.telegraph.co.uk/travel/news/ryanair/Ryanair-worst-brand-for-customer-service/

3   *Daily Mail* (2014, 30 October). No more Mr Meanie! Retrieved from www. dailymail.co.uk/travel/travel_news/article-2813863/Controversial-Ryanair-boss-admits-no-frills-carrier-nicer-customers-sooner.html

4   Southwest Airlines. *About Southwest*. Retrieved from www.southwest.com/html/about-southwest/

5   Hamel, G. (2012). *What Matters Now. How to Win in a World of Relentless Change, Ferocious Competition, and Unstoppable Innovation*. Jossy-Bass.

6   Schwartz, N. (2006, October 2). BP was warned. *Fortune*. Retrieved from http://archive.fortune.com/2006/10/02/magazines/fortune/BP_leak_short.fortune/index.htm

7   Salz, A (2013). An Independent Review of Barclays Business Practices.

8   *BBC News* (2012, 3 July). Profile: Barclays' chief executive Bob Diamond. Retrieved from www.bbc.co.uk/news/business-18625227

9   Business in the Community. (2013, 18 December). Barclays Group Chief Executive Antony Jenkins to become new Business in the Community Chairman. Retrievedfromwww.bitc.org.uk/news-events/news/barclays-group-chief-executive-antony-jenkins-become-new-business-community

10 Ruddick, G. & Kollewe, J. (2017, 10 April). Barclays boss used bank's security team to hunt for whistleblower. *The Guardian*. Retrieved from www.theguardian.com/business/2017/apr/10/barclays-boss-jes-staley-may-lose-bonus-over-bid-to-expose-whistleblower

11 Groceries Code Adjudicator (2016, 26 January). Investigation into Tesco plc. Retrieved from www.gov.uk/government/uploads/system/uploads/attachment_data/file/494840/GCA_Tesco_plc_final_report_26012016_-_version_for_download.pdf

12 Drucker, P. (2007). *Essential Drucker: Classic Drucker Collection*. Routledge.

13 Jones II, P.T. (2015, 16 April). *Why we need to rethink capitalism*. Ted Talks. Retrieved from www.youtube.com/watch?v=dvJSK4viVMs

14 The B Team & Virgin Unite. (2015). *New Ways of Working*. Retrieved from www.tvwleadershipacademy.nhs.uk/sites/default/files/5.%20New%20Ways%20of%20Working%20(B%20Team%20%26%20Virgin%20Unite%202015)_0.pdf

15 The B Team & Virgin Unite. (2015). *New Ways of Working*. Retrieved from www.tvwleadershipacademy.nhs.uk/sites/default/files/5.%20New%20Ways%20of%20Working%20(B%20Team%20%26%20Virgin%20Unite%202015)_0.pdf

16 Nielsen. (2015).Consumer-goods' Brands that Demonstrate Commitment to Sustainability Outperform those that don't [Press Release]. Retrieved from www.nielsen.com/ug/en/press-room/2015/consumer-goods-brands-that-demonstrate-commitment-to-sustainability-outperform.html

17 Edelman (2017). *Edelman Trust Barometer: Annual Global Study*. Retrieved from www.edelman.com/trust2017/

18 Harvard Business Review. Introverts, Extroverts, and the Complexities of Team Dynamics. March 16, 2015. https://hbr.org/2015/03/introverts-extroverts-and-the-complexities-of-team-dynamics

19 Edelman (2016). *Edelman Trust Barometer Global Survey*. Retrieved from www.edelman.com/insights/intellectual-property/2016-edelman-trust-barometer/

20 Edelman (2017). *Edelman Trust Barometer: Annual Global Study*. Retrieved from www.edelman.com/trust2017/

21 Hamel, G. (2012). *What Matters Now. How to Win in a World of Relentless Change, Ferocious Competition, and Unstoppable Innovation*. Jossy-Bass.

Chapter 4

1   Huffington Post (2009, 24 August). 'United Breaks Guitars': Did It Really Cost The Airline $180 Million? *The Huffington Post*. Retrieved from www. huffingtonpost.com/2009/07/24/united-breaks-guitars-did_n_244357.html

2   Facebook. @zafirafires. Retrieved from www.facebook.com/Zafirafires/posts/1511757242454601

3   Evans, J (2015, 23 November). Vauxhall Zafira fires: is DVSA car safety regulator fit for purpose? *The Sunday Times: Driving*. Retrieved from www. driving.co.uk/news/vauxhall-zafira-fires-is-dvsa-the-car-safety-regulator-fit-for-purpose/

4   The B Team & Virgin Unite. (2015). *New Ways of Working*. Retrieved from www.tvwleadershipacademy.nhs.uk/sites/default/files/5.%20New%20 Ways%20of%20Working%20(B%20Team%20%26%20Virgin%20 Unite%202015)_0.pdf

5   Institute for the Future. (2007). *The Future of Work. The Intersection of Work and Technology*. Retrieved from www.iftf.org/uploads/media/FOW_map_screen.pdf

6   Edelman (2017). *Edelman Trust Barometer: Annual Global Study*. Retrieved from www.edelman.com/trust2017/

7   Poushter, J. (2015). *Measuring the 'Good' Life Around the World*. Pew Research Centre. Retrieved from www.pewresearch.org/fact-tank/2015/10/29/ measuring-the-good-life-around-the-world/

8   Salem, F. & Mourtada, R. (2011) *Arab Social Media Report*. Dubai School of Government. Retrieved from http://unpan1.un.org/intradoc/groups/public/ documents/dsg/unpan044212.pdf

9   Lapowsky, I (2016, 19 August). The Man Behind Trump's Bid to Finally Take Digital Seriously. *Wired*. Retrieved from www.wired.com/2016/08/ man-behind-trumps-bid-finally-take-digital-seriously/

10 Issacson, W. (2015). *Steve Jobs: The Exclusive Biography*. Abacus.

11 IBM's 100 Icons of Progress. Retrieved from www-03.ibm.com/ibm/history/ ibm100/us/en/icons/

Chapter 5

1   Montgomery, A. (2014, 1 April). Wally Olins dies aged 83. *Design week*. Retrieved from www.designweek.co.uk/issues/april-2014/wally-olins-dies-aged-83/

2   Olins, W. (2004). *On Brand*. Thames & Hudson.

3   Klein, N. (1999). *No Logo*. Harper Collins.

4   Trout, J. (2004). *Trout on Strategy*. McGraw Hill.

5   Murray, K. (2013).*The Language of Leaders: How Top CEOs Communicate to Inspire, Influence and Achieve Results*. Kogan Press.

6   Ipsos Global Reputation Centre (2015). *The Reputation Council, Latest Findings from the Tenth Sitting*. Retrieved from www.ipsos.com/sites/default/ files/Ipsos_Reputation_Council_2015_Report.pdf

7   Edelman (2016). *Edelman Trust Barometer Global Survey*. Retrieved from www.edelman.com/insights/intellectual-property/2016-edelman-trust-barometer/

8   Edelman (2016). *Edelman Trust Barometer Global Survey*. Retrieved from www.edelman.com/insights/intellectual-property/2016-edelman-trust-barometer/

9   Ipsos Global Reputation Centre (2015). *The Reputation Council, Latest Findings from the Tenth Sitting.* Retrieved from www.ipsos.com/sites/default/files/Ipsos_Reputation_Council_2015_Report.pdf

10 Eccles, R., Newquist, S., & Schatz, R. (2007). *Reputation and its Risks.* Harvard Business Review.

11 Branson, R. (2013). *Screw Business as Usual.* Virgin Books.

Chapter 6

1   Gallup. (2013). *State of the Global Workplace Report.* Retrieved from www.gallup.com/services/178517/state-global-workplace.aspx

2   Gladwell, M. (2000). *Tipping Point: How Little Things can make a Big Difference.* Abacus.

3   Gonsalves, R. (2016, 24 November). The end of fast fashion? The man bringing high quality basics back to the high street. *The Telegraph.* Retrieved from www.telegraph.co.uk/fashion/brands/end-fast-fashion-man-bringing-high-quality-basics-back-high/

Part 3

1   Berlin, I. (1953). *The Hedgehog and the Fox.* Weidenfeld & Nicolson.

2   Collins, J. (2001). *Good to Great.* Random House Business.

Chapter 7

1   Hodgkinson, G., & Starbuck, W. (2012). *The Oxford Handbook of Organizational Decision Making.* Oxford University Press.

2   *Financial Times* (2004, 15 September). Not to Mince Words. Retrieved from www.ft.com/cms/s/0/4970b6a0-06b3-11d9-b95e-00000e2511c8.html?ft_site=falcon&desktop=true#axzz4e1QQJob4

3   Surowiecki, J. (2005). *The Wisdom of Crowds: Why the Many Are Smarter Than the Few.* Abacus.

4   Leadbetter, C. (2009). *We-Think.* Profile Books.

5   Pearson (2015). *Transforming our impact: Pearson sustainability report, 2015.* Retrieved from www.pearson.com/content/dam/one-dot-com/one-dot-com/global/Files/sustainability/2015-report/full-2015-report.pdf

6   Steve Jobs Oldie but Goodie. Retrieved from www.youtube.com/watch?v=vmG9jzCHtSQ

Chapter 8

No references

Chapter 9

1   Drucker, P. (2007). *Essential Drucker: Classic Drucker Collection.* Routledge.

2   Balmer, J.M.T. & Soenen, G.M. (1999). The Acid Test of Corporate Identity Management™. *Journal of Marketing Management* 15(1-3) pp.69-92. Retreived from www.tandfonline.com/doi/abs/10.1362/026725799784870441

3   Browne, J. (2015). *Connect: How Companies Succeed by Radically Engaging with Society.* Penguin Random House.

4   GRI, The UN Global Compact, & The World Business Council for Sustainable Development (WBCSD). (2016). *SDG Compass, The Guide for Business Action on the SDGs.* Retrieved from http://sdgcompass.org/wp-content/ uploads/2015/12/019104_SDG_Compass_Guide_2015.pdf
5   World Wildlife Fund (2016). Palmoil buyers scorecard 2016. Retrieved from http://palmoilscorecard.panda.org/check-the-scores/manufacturers/unilever
6   Webb, J. (2016, 30 November). Amnesty International Slams Colgate, Nestlé and Unilever For Palm Oil Supply Chain Abuses. *Forbes.* Retrieved from www. forbes.com/sites/jwebb/2016/11/30/amnesty-international-slams-colgate-nestle-and-unilever-for-palm-oil-supply-chain-abuses/#1470fb514ea3

Chapter 10

1   Ghemawat, P. (1991). *Commitment: The Dynamic of Strategy.* Macmillan.
2   Schein, E. H. (2010). Organizational Culture and Leadership. Jossey-Bass.
3   Byers, M., Coerver, H. (2013) *Road to Relevance.* ASAE Association Management Press.
4   De Beers (2014). *Turning Finite Resources into Enduring Opportunity.* De Beers, 2014.

Index

Please note that page references to Figures will be in *italics*. 'SOI' stands for 'Single Organizing Idea'.

 Taylor & Francis eBooks

---

Helping you to choose the right eBooks for your Library

Add Routledge titles to your library's digital collection today. Taylor and Francis ebooks contains over 50,000 titles in the Humanities, Social Sciences, Behavioural Sciences, Built Environment and Law.

Choose from a range of subject packages or create your own!

Benefits for you

» Free MARC records
» COUNTER-compliant usage statistics
» Flexible purchase and pricing options
» All titles DRM-free.

REQUEST YOUR FREE INSTITUTIONAL TRIAL TODAY

Free Trials Available
We offer free trials to qualifying academic, corporate and government customers.

Benefits for your user

» Off-site, anytime access via Athens or referring URL
» Print or copy pages or chapters
» Full content search
» Bookmark, highlight and annotate text
» Access to thousands of pages of quality research at the click of a button.

eCollections – Choose from over 30 subject eCollections, including:

Archaeology	Language Learning
Architecture	Law
Asian Studies	Literature
Business & Management	Media & Communication
Classical Studies	Middle East Studies
Construction	Music
Creative & Media Arts	Philosophy
Criminology & Criminal Justice	Planning
Economics	Politics
Education	Psychology & Mental Health
Energy	Religion
Engineering	Security
English Language & Linguistics	Social Work
Environment & Sustainability	Sociology
Geography	Sport
Health Studies	Theatre & Performance
History	Tourism, Hospitality & Events

For more information, pricing enquiries or to order a free trial, please contact your local sales team:
www.tandfebooks.com/page/sales

 Routledge
Taylor & Francis Group

The home of
Routledge books

www.tandfebooks.com